Praise for A High Impact LIFE

"This book is an unwavering effort to restore what has been lost in how we do life and business. A High Impact LIFE reinforces God's unique purpose for our lives. As we pursue that purpose, with a passion, we will see the High Impact we can have on our families, businesses, and our communities."
-David Green, Founder, Hobby Lobby

"Get ready to be challenged. No more excuses. If you want a High Impact Life, this is your road map. Ochs provides a framework for how to understand your purpose and a plan for its achievement. This will be a book you will love to read and if you do what it suggests, a book that will change your life."
- Chad Edwards, Senior VP, Young Life

"As one of the inmates who Pete spent these past 10 years walking with, I am excited to have all of his advice in one book. I am no longer incarcerated, but Pete continues to be an important part of my future. Reading this book has once again caused me to reevaluate my own Purpose, Passion and Platform. Thank you, Pete."
- Randal Pennington, Ex-Offender

"By the time I was half way through I noticed the book had gotten bigger? I had underlined almost every page and folded the corner in as an indication something great was written on that page....A High Impact LIFE is a fantastic read. Pete is able to get into the mind of the reader and help him/her explore what he/she hadn't thought of yet on the journey."
- Durell Miller, Businessman

Multiply your Impact by Changing your Habits

High Impact Habits is the curriculum that will help you practically apply what you are learning in A High Impact LIFE.

High Impact Habits when used with *A High Impact LIFE* will:

- Help you create your own personal **LIFE PLAN**
- Teach you the power of **WEEKLY STRATEGY** so you focus on the important and not the urgent
- Train you in the habit of **DAILY EXECUTION** to maximize your productivity and peace of mind

FOR PERSONAL OR SMALL GROUP USE

www.EnterpriseStewardship.com

A HIGH IMPACT LIFE

LOVE YOUR **PURPOSE**
LIVE WITH **PASSION**
LEVERAGE YOUR **PLATFORM**

ENTERPRISE STEWARDSHIP
——— EQUIPPING STEWARD LEADERS ———

Pete Ochs

Thank You

Deb, for being a great partner in our journey of faith, family, friends, and fun.

Austin and Danielle, Jon and Lauren, for making family a little bit of heaven on earth.

Mom and Dad, for giving me foundational values based on Truth.

Bill, for being the big brother I never had and the consummate example of a high impact LIFE.

Bob, Dave, and Jed for exemplifying to me, true, sacrificial friendship.

George, Howard, and Marvin who have mentored me with their humble doses of wisdom.

Daryl, Jess, Joe, Tom, and Wes for inspiration and accountability.

Austin, Josh, Jose, Nick, Roddy and all the Capital III team who have redefined the purpose of business.

The Inmates at HCF who have proven that flourishing can occur in the most difficult situations.

The Trinity Academy family who have demonstrated the power of Truth, Faith, and Character.

And Jesus, who is the Author and Perfecter of faith, service, excellence, and stewardship.

Love your Purpose.
Live with Passion.
Leverage your
Platform.

Pete Ochs

TABLE OF CONTENTS

Introduction..I

LOVE YOUR PURPOSE
Chapter 1
If Success Doesn't Bring Satisfaction Then What Does?......................1
Chapter 2
It's All About Having The Right Why.................................... 19
Chapter 3
Finding My ultimate Purpose- Honoring God..........................39

LIVE WITH PASSION
Chapter 4
The Greatest Calling - Serving People....................................77
Chapter 5
The Highest Standard - Pursuing Excellence.........................113
Chapter 6
The Ultimate Career - Stewarding Capital..............................13

LEVERAGE YOUR PLATFORM
Chapter 7
Created to Flourish...167
Chapter 8
High Impact Life..201

SCRIPTURE ANNOTATIONS....................................213

ABOUT THE AUTHOR..234

It's about a day-to-day, lifelong journey that is not just a commitment to DO better but BE better.

Pete Ochs

INTRODUCTION

Do you want to make a difference?

D o you want it to matter that you lived? If your answer is yes, we have something in common: we both want a high-impact life that will make the world a better place.

This journey started for me twenty-five years ago when I turned forty. That milestone caused me to sit up and take a little extra notice of where I was in life. As I pondered my lack of satisfaction with what I had achieved, I came to the realization that I had spent virtually all my first forty years chasing the elusive American dream: success defined by personal accomplishment, social standing, and financial security. And although the number of zeros in my accounts did not reach the dizzying heights of some, I achieved enough success to discover that the dream could not deliver the satisfaction I wanted. Not then, not ever. And so began my pursuit of a more satisfying life. I soon discovered that although my work itself created some level of fulfillment, the results of my work – personal accomplishment, social standing, and financial security – were not very satisfying. The journey was more rewarding than the destination.

For the first time in my life I began to ask those uncomfortable, penetrating questions. What's my purpose? What am I passionate about? What's my calling? And that all-encompassing question: Why do I exist? Over the next several months, I experienced a mixture of mental, emotional, and spiritual turmoil, punctuated with a few aha moments. I spent intentional time alone in personal reflection, time with God in prayer, and time with mentors in concerted conversation. What I found was the clarity my life had been lacking. Beliefs and ideas that I had vaguely acknowledged began to become clear, solidifying in my mind.

All this led me to one clear and unequivocal conclusion – my purpose in life was not to live for myself but to live for something greater. That simple commitment changed my life. I told God that from that day forward I would strive to live like a steward and not an owner. Everything I had would be considered His and I would steward it as faithfully as I could.

My purpose in life was not to live for myself but to live for something greater.

For the next ten years I strove to be the best steward I could be. But for all my good intentions, I could not escape slipping back into my old ways of living. Although I had moved from creating wealth for myself to creating wealth for God's kingdom, it was still about me and what I was creating. I measured my self-worth by my net worth. I measured my standing in God's sight by the amount of financial assets I could contribute to His work. I had become satisfied and prideful of what I was doing for God.

At the age of fifty, I faced another life changing moment: 9/11.

After the attacks of September 11, 2001, our businesses went into a precipitous downturn. Sales declined. Profits became losses. Cash evaporated. Financial generosity disappeared. Hope turned to disillusionment. And once again I questioned the meaning of life. I questioned the sovereignty of God. I can remember those early mornings when I repeatedly asked, "Lord, don't You understand all the good things I have done for You? Don't You understand how generous I have been to You?"

After another intense time of introspection, the answer came back loud and clear. "Pete, I don't want your money, I want you." You see, ten years earlier when I had committed to be a steward instead of an owner, my head and my heart were sincere. But over time, my pride and my desire to control crept back in. I had simply replaced the pride of profits with the pride of generosity. Although my heart wanted to replace the desire for success with the commitment to live a surrendered life, over time I wound up in the mushy middle: one foot in the world of success and the other in the kingdom of surrender. As a result, I coexisted in the lukewarm world of what I call "satisfied significance." I was neither hot nor cold. I had become satisfied. I assuaged my worldly pride with kingdom generosity, but in the end it was still about me. Through this struggle, God helped me learn another life lesson: the attainment of a high-impact life is not a destination but a journey. It's not about a six-month exercise that results in becoming a better person. It's about a day-to-day, lifelong journey that is not just a commitment to do better but to be better. It is a striving to know God on a personal,

The attainment of a high-impact life is not a destination but a journey.

surrendered, sacrificial level. And it's a journey that will not end until the day we meet our Creator, face to face. Ten years earlier I had learned that living for me was not as satisfying as living for something greater than myself. I had been great at doing but I had failed to be the man God wanted me to be. The problem was that God didn't just want my head and my hands; He wanted my heart. He wanted me to become a son with a deep personal relationship with Him built on faith and trust.

With this new heart change and renewed passion, I began to make changes in the way I lived my life. The greatest change came in how I viewed my business. I had always considered my business as a tool to create financial assets that I could use personally or invest to further God's purposes in the world. It was a transactional enterprise, managed with the intent of creating economic capital. As I began to experience personal transformation, as my world-view shifted from living for me to living for something greater, I began to see our business not just as an economic engine but as a platform to impact people in ways far beyond the reach of financial wealth.

While I was going through this personal transformation, we were presented with a business opportunity that would change my life. This opportunity meant moving part of our manufacturing operations behind the walls of a maximum-security prison. As crazy as it sounded, we decided to pursue this venture because we were having difficulty hiring enough manufacturing labor for a rapidly expanding business. Full disclosure: this move was initially made for purely financial reasons. Here was a work force that was ready made, would work hard, and would show up on time every day! But I soon learned that God moved us to this prison environment for much more than a steady labor supply; He was about to teach me how to live out my faith in the marketplace. Behind these prison walls I found a group of men who had been stripped of everything you and I would consider essential. They had lost their freedom to work, which destroyed their ability to provide financially for themselves and their families. They had lost their dignity and the self-worth that comes from working hard for a day's pay. They had lost their freedom to live and contribute alongside their fellow man for the purpose of promoting the common good. And many of them had come to the place where they had lost their way morally. Their lack of an overarching purpose in life resulted in no moral code by which to determine right from wrong. They were living in a state of economic, social, and spiritual poverty.

As I came to understand this dilemma, it convicted me to become a person who would make a difference. By spending time with these men, I realized that they were not much different from you and me. They had been publicly stripped of all their pride, pleasure, and possessions; but their hopes and dreams were the same as ours. They had lost the things that can allow you and me to hide from dealing with the important questions in life. They were broken and open and honest.

And so we set out on a grand journey, a great experiment to see if we could create holistic wealth from economic, social, and spiritual poverty. We sought nothing less than to create human flourishing in a desert that required us to invest our excess economic, social, and spiritual wealth in the needs of those less fortunate.

I've spent the last ten years of my life walking with these men, and it has changed me profoundly. Through them I am finally learning not only to do but to be. I am experiencing what it means to love the Lord with my head, my heart, and my hands, and to love my neighbor as myself. And I am beginning to understand the power and enjoyment of loving my purpose, living with passion, and leveraging my platform. As I began to dig deeper into this trilogy of Purpose, Passion, and Platform, I began to display graphically what God was teaching me. I invite you to join me in a transformative journey that follows our Impact Framework.

The framework incorporates three triangles. I define the center "Honor God" triangle as our Purpose in life. The three surrounding triangles labeled Serve People, Pursue Excellence, and Steward Capital, represent our Passions in life. And the outline of the triangle represents our Platform in life and bears the words Economic, Social, and Spiritual.

Over the next few chapters we will begin to unpack the lessons God has been teaching me. My prayer is that this journey will encourage and challenge each of us to create a world of human flourishing by loving our purpose, living with passion, and leveraging our platform.

Welcome to the journey.

Pete Ochs

God does not want your attempt at perfection, He simply wants your heart.

Lauren Rolph

Chapter 1

IF SUCCESS DOESN'T BRING SATISFACTION THEN WHAT DOES?

"The unexamined life is not worth living"

Socrates

A FEW YEARS AGO, I WAS ASKED TO do the eulogy at the funeral of one of my best friends. I was moved and challenged at the thought of speaking about the high-impact life my friend had lived. As I pondered what I could say about him, it forced me to contemplate what others might say about me at my memorial service. A sobering thought.

What about you? What would your friends say? If they were to give an honest account, how would they describe you and your life? Would they talk about your success and accomplishments, or would they recall warmly how you had lived for something greater than yourself? Would it be about how you had advanced yourself or how you had served others? Would it be about what you had accumulated and the possessions you owned, or would it be about your generous spirit and what you gave away?

As I pondered what my friends might say, my eulogy preparation became even more challenging. A massive question overwhelmed me: What would the Creator of the universe say about me? Would He consider me a good steward of the time, talent and treasure He had allowed me to manage? Trying to answer this question, of course, meant breaking it down into a parade of sub-questions. How would God assess the time I spent here on earth? Had I been a good steward of the time He had entrusted to me? What about my talents? Did I invest them faithfully? And then the zinger: What about my treasure? Did I really "seek first His kingdom"?

Here's the bottom line. At the end of my life, I want to stand before the God of the universe and hear Him say, "Well done, good and faithful servant." If God greets me at heaven's gates with those words, I know that I, like my friend, will have lived a high-impact life – the life of the good and faithful steward.

I believe the essence of a high-impact life is to know with your head, believe with your heart, and work with your hands to fulfill the purpose, passion, and platform God has designed for you. Over the next few chapters, we will unpack these concepts together; purpose, passion, and platform.

SUCCESS VERSUS SATISFACTION

To set the stage, I want to ask you the question that God asked me on my fortieth birthday, the question that He used to launch me on my search for this high-impact life.

"Why doesn't success bring satisfaction?"

I woke up on my fortieth birthday and realized that while I had become successful by the world's standards, I was deeply dissatisfied. This reality just didn't make any sense to me; it didn't seem to square with my life's resume.

As the son of a farmer and a school teacher, I had been blessed to have a family that gave the first ten percent, saved the next ten percent, and lived on the balance. Hard work, integrity, and individual responsibility had been burned into my soul.

Not surprisingly, my forty-year resume looked strong. Financially, I was independent, fulfilling a lifelong goal. I had started Capital III, an investment banking company acting as the intermediary in private-company transactions. After several years we began to acquire our own portfolio of companies, which provided financial security and social standing.

Socially, we had a great family. We raised two kids who were successful in their own right. They married well and had kids, and I had the pleasure of my son joining me in business. We were blessed with a terrific group of friends and lived in a close-knit, safe, midwestern town – a bit insulated from the trials and tribulations many people in the world face.

Spiritually, we attended church regularly and I lived what I considered to be a good Christian life. I said and did the right things and people affirmed me in my good deeds and obvious spiritual earnestness. I volunteered in several ministries and was proud of my community involvement.

We had it all. Or so it seemed. So, why the dissatisfaction? With a troubled spirit, I began a process of inner reflection. I prayed, talked to friends, included my wife in examining every facet of my life, and spent time reading the usual books on the subject. Slowly, the pieces began to fall into place. And the picture was disturbing. All my pursuits of success shared a common measuring stick, and that measuring stick was ME. My pursuit of success was nothing more than a desire to build a life that was all about me.

That realization jolted me – a seismic shock that upended my worldview. For the first time I questioned my true motive in life. The honest answer? I was living for myself. I had mastered the ability to shroud it in a bit of feigned humility and self-deprecation, but at the end of the day, it was about me. You see, I was intently focused on who I was, how I lived, and what I owned. Here's what I learned. The focus on who I was manifested itself in my pursuit of being a successful entrepreneur. My self-worth was tied to what I had accomplished as a businessman. My definition of success was exceeding the success of other businessmen in town. I had great pride in who people thought I was. It was also very important to me that people thought of me as a good person. My "goodness" was everywhere to be seen: great wife, great kids, good friends, good relationships, good citizen. I worked hard to build a reputation of honesty and character. There was one more important "goodness": by the world's standards I was a good Christian. Most Sunday mornings you would find me in church. I volunteered in several ministries. I occasionally prayed and even read my Bible. If you would have asked people who I was, most would have said I was a good person. Although they wouldn't have added this, the truth is that I was a very proud person.

Pride drove the identity I was building for myself. Pride has a way of working itself deeper into our spirit. Soon, it wasn't just about having pride in who I was, but it spread to the pleasure I derived from how I lived. And it showed. I possessed all the trappings of a successful entrepreneur: European car, nice house in a nice neighborhood, member of the country club. My kids attended private school and all my friends were successful businessmen.

Oh, I maintained a spiritual life, but it was more of a Sunday morning thing. My relationship with God was sporadic at best. Sometimes deep and meaningful but often superficial and short lived. My first waking thoughts on most mornings were about furthering my personal ambitions, my reputation, and my lifestyle. I lived a very comfortable, pleasure-seeking life.

From there, the final step in this 'pride slide' was easy. The pride of who I was and how I lived led inevitably to a pride in what I owned. I worked diligently to make sure my business went beyond financial success. I wanted my net worth to reach those mystical levels that would allow me to join the millionaire club. Money became a major driver for me. But it wasn't really the money, it was what it bought: stature, respect, admiration, pleasure, and security.

Even though accumulation of wealth drove me, I always considered myself a generous person. We gave away ten percent of our income, but there was little joy in it. As I think back, this ritual was probably more about a discipline I learned as a child rather than a heartfelt offering to the Creator of the universe. It was something I considered a necessary obligation as a Christian. I took great pride (there it is again) in the fact that I was a 90/10 guy. I wanted to make a lot of money so that my ten percent to God was a big number. Well, you can imagine what I had planned for the ninety percent. I would be "generous" with the ten percent as long as God left me and my ninety percent alone. After all, I was a guy who loved his possessions.

THE WORLD OF ME

How did I get to be so focused on myself, my needs, wants, and ambitions? Where did the pride come from and why was it so hard to address? I think the problem for most of us is that we let the world define for us what is a successful and satisfying life. And the world defines it as a life centered around who I am, how I live, and what I own. We live in a world that is all about ME.

Look around you; it is everywhere! From professional sports to the entertainment industry to politics and even the church – pride drives us. We witness a constant parade of people who desire to be in the limelight, to be admired and even envied. And despite so much evidence to the contrary, we actually do envy them, believing that they are happier and more satisfied than we are.

In my world, it is the pride of business ownership that drives so many. Do whatever makes the next quarterly earnings look better, no matter how immoral or unethical it may be. Our motto has become: I've worked hard for it, I deserve it, it's mine, and no one is going to take it from me. It's the American way. Life is about me. It's about who I am, how I live, and what I own.

Unfortunately, the fixation with the American dream starts early in life. We become indoctrinated at birth. Parents live vicariously through their kids, pushing and promoting them to be super scholars and athletes so they might achieve what their parents never could. Our educational system exacerbates the problem, promising that the next diploma is the ticket to our dream job. From birth to graduation, we are set up to join the relentless march toward the world's definition of success. And all along the way the carrots dangled in front of us are the chance to "be" somebody (the who); to live the way we want, making our own choices and controlling our own destiny (the how); and to buy all the things that will bring us happiness (the what). It's what drove me. Can you identify with my predicament?

I had made my platform my purpose for living.

I had made the ultimate mistake: I had made my platform my purpose for living. Unfortunately, this kind of mistake isn't limited to the world of business success. All of us, regardless of our gifting and passion, are subject to confusing our platform with our purpose. Consider Lauren Rolph, a spouse and mom, who wrote this about her experience.

> *Tears streamed down my face as I stared at a glowing sonogram of our eight-week-old baby. No heartbeat. This would be our second miscarriage in six months. And it would not be our last.*

> *As a little girl, my dreams of the future always included being a mom. Growing up with a strong sense of family was incredibly valuable to me. But in this moment, my hope for a future family had been replaced with grief; my joy, with despair.*

> *In my pain and sadness, I was angry with the Lord. It had felt cruel for the Lord to give and take away. I was guilt stricken and ashamed for feeling angry with Him, but questions and doubts kept filling my mind.*

> *Will I ever have kids? How could this happen? Is the Lord who He says He is? Is this a punishment? What did I do wrong?*

> *I had always strived to please and honor the Lord – to read my*

Bible, memorize Scripture, be prayerful – but it never seemed to be enough. In my humanity I never seemed to get it "right." Without realizing it, I had begun to believe the lie that my purpose was in my performance. What I accomplished for the Lord would somehow determine His love for me. It was an exhausting and unattainable goal I would never reach. In my corrupted view, if the Lord's love depended on my faithfulness, then the pain I was experiencing must be a punishment. And now in my sadness, I had no real desire to pursue the Lord; instead, I was deeply angry with Him. I never imagined getting to this point.

This is where the beauty of my story begins. Here in this sadness, ugly anger, and hopelessness, the Lord met me. How was I going to embrace the joy and love of the Lord in the depth of my pain? He was not threatened by my emotions or my doubt; instead, He wanted to meet me right there in the midst of them. God is our redeemer and it's by the way of the cross, the way of pain, that He wants to heal us.

In *The Chronicles of Narnia*, by C.S. Lewis, someone asks if Aslan, the lion, is safe. "Who said anything about safe? Course he isn't safe. But he's good. He's the King, I tell you."

Life with God doesn't always feel safe, but He is good. At the time, I didn't feel that He was either safe or good.

As I struggled through that season, the Lord healed my heart to trust that He is good even when it doesn't feel like it. He was leading me to let go of the expectations, guilt, and pressures I had put on myself. I wanted to be enough and I was constantly coming up short. I began to see that in His mercy, the Lord was pursuing me time and time again – even when I wasn't pursuing Him. Over and over the Lord kept communicating to me, "I love you not for what you do but *for who you are: you are My child, a child of God."*

I began to truly believe in a deeper way than ever before that I am a child of God. That I am enough. I have enough. Because Jesus is enough. When we surrender to Jesus, we are set free.

My purpose in life changed: it was no longer about what I could do for the Lord, but about who He is and who I am in Him. The Lord does not want my attempt at perfection; He simply wants my heart. My purpose is to live free and flourish as a child of God. This freedom and flourishing began to spill into all aspects of my life.

Over the next several years I came to be the momma of eight babies. Three ended up in heaven after only moments in my life, but they had changed my life forever. Five were born over the next seven years. As I began my journey of motherhood filled with joy and gratitude, I was surprised to find that it would also be overshadowed by mom guilt and the burden of the mundane.

Mom guilt: I think every mother has felt it. From the moment a baby is born there is an incredible amount of pressure. There are thousands of questions and insecurities. Am I doing this right? The same lie I had believed earlier in my life began to creep back in: If I do things "right," life will look a certain way. If I feed my kids the right things, they will never be sick. If I manage their schedule, they will sleep through the night.

This is not reality. Life happens, and we live in an imperfect world. "In this world you will have trouble. But take heart! I have overcome the world" (John 16:33). My newfound purpose transformed the way I viewed my new platform of being a mom and wife. If I desired to see my children flourish and live free, then I needed to model it for them. The truth was sinking in and I was able to receive God's grace and begin walking in His freedom. This became my passion for being a mom.

Burden of the mundane: Life as a mom can feel mundane. Laundry, dirty dishes, runny noses . . . there is never an end. What am I doing that really matters in this mundane existence? Rather than feeling like a grand mission for the Lord, motherhood sometimes feels ordinary and insignificant, but the Lord called me to surrender to the idea that He is found in the beauty of the everyday.

Success to me is no longer having done some amazing thing for the Lord — having the perfect marriage, family, or job. Success is in surrender, and that is where I found contentment. Surrendering to the platform the Lord has given me, recognizing the unique set of gifts and abilities He has placed in me, loving and serving the people He has put in front of me — all of these help me to accomplish with love and excellence the tasks He has ordained for me. My kids are experiencing the love of Jesus when I make the millionth peanut butter and jelly sandwich, put a band-aid on their latest ouchie, or when I offer a shoulder to cry on. The Lord is in the present. Love has the power to make the ordinary something special.

Success is in surrender, and that is where I found contentment.

I daily need reminding of the truth. Living out my faith and humanity can often look messy. But there is beauty in the struggle, a freedom from perfection, a call to purpose, an abundance of grace. And there is Jesus. It is by His wounds we are healed. When my

---

HIGH IMPACT HABIT
God does not want your attempt at perfection, He simply wants your heart.

---

struggle meets the reality of the cross and who Jesus is, I can live free and flourish as a child of God.

Please take a moment to reread Lauren's last paragraph. There is such power in those words when we routinely remind ourselves of the truth.

CHASING THE THREE P'S

In my early years, I became friends with a successful businessman. He gave me this advice for how to become successful in business: "Pete, pursue the magic formula of pride, pleasure, and profitability. Make sure every business deal you do contains these three elements." It didn't take me very long to figure out that this wasn't very sound advice. He died several years ago, humbled, sad, and financially bankrupt. Yet his advice seems to be the bedrock of our American culture.

So why have we become so fixated on self? Let me posit a simple reason: we have become focused on the created instead of the Creator. When we become economically and materialistically successful, we become self-reliant. That's exactly what happened to me. Can you relate?

This self-reliance always results in living for me instead of something greater than me. I believe it is the result of moving from a theonomous (God centered) culture to an autonomous (me centered) culture. In a theonomous culture, we are governed by a set of laws that come from a higher power. God is first; we are second. In an autonomous culture, I determine the rules. Humanity reigns supreme, while God is relegated to second place if He is even acknowledged at all. God himself has something to say about a theonomous culture compared to an autonomous one. 2000 years ago, one of Jesus' disciples, John, wrote about this very problem. Yes, this is not just an American phenomenon. It has been around for centuries. Here is what John had to say: *"Do not love the world or anything in the world . . . for everything in the world, the cravings of sinful man, the lust of his eyes and the boasting of what he has and does, comes not from the Father but from the world." (1 John 2:15-16, NIV 1984)*

He nailed it. Those three Ps my business friend lived by were already a problem in the first-century church – and well before that. The *"cravings of sinful man"* are about what I own, my possessions. John warns us not to be possessed by our possessions. Yet we buy things we don't need with money we don't have to impress people we don't even like. This is the power these "cravings" can have in our lives.

The *"lust of his eyes"* is about how I live. It measures success in terms of personal pleasure. In 2016, Americans spent over $500 billion on entertainment, three times as much as we spent on education. There is a cost to this unbridled pursuit: 80 percent of our current healthcare costs are related to the addictions of smoking, obesity, drugs, and alcohol. This is the "fruit" of indulging the lust of the eyes.

Finally, the *"boasting of what he has and does"* is all about who I am. It's about a pride-driven thirst for those things that prop up our self-esteem and further our self-centered worldview. It is also the primary source of our fear, our stress, our discouragement and, ultimately, our despair. That is the reward for a life of "boasting of what [we have and do]."

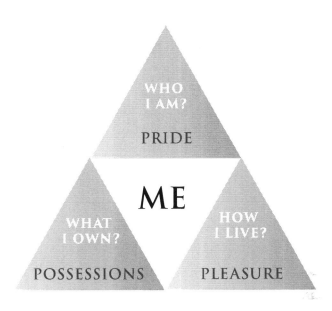

Below is a graphical representation of a life that is centered around me with a focus on pride, pleasure, and possessions.

The result of chasing the three Ps of pride, pleasure, and possessions is a dissatisfied life. I woke up after 20 years of the chase and realized that the thrill of the three Ps lasts for only a moment. That moment may be powerful, but the law of diminishing returns kept shrinking it; the more I achieved, the shorter that moment lasted. My me-centered lifestyle resulted in exactly the opposite of what I really wanted. My goal was happiness and contentment, but my reality was total dissatisfaction.

Have you experienced this as well? Has a new car or a new job or a bigger house ever provided the satisfaction you had hoped for? Have you been pursuing the who, how and what of life, only to be left as dissatisfied as I was? Then lean in, because there is good news coming. But first, I need to introduce you to the BIG question.

WHY ASK WHY?

Several years ago we had a very important event in our family, the wedding of my only daughter. The ceremony and everything leading up to it had gone smoothly. Then came the reception and the moment to cut the beautiful multitiered cake. With video rolling and cameras flashing, my daughter and son-in-law took the knife, raised it dramatically, and tried to slice the cake. But the cake wouldn't slice. Puzzled, they looked at each other and tried again. Still, the knife couldn't cut the cake. It took them a moment, but then you could see in their eyes that the lights had come on. They moved the knife up to a higher tier on the cake and, voila! The cake cut perfectly. The problem was that the bottom two layers of the cake weren't cake. They were cardboard! They looked like cake. They smelled like cake. The frosting even tasted like cake. Everyone thought it was cake. But it wasn't cake!

That is the perfect metaphor for my life at forty – all frosting and no cake. I had worked hard to look great on the outside but on the inside, things were hollow. I have learned that if we focus only on the frosting – on the three Ps of pride, pleasure, and possessions (*who* we are, *how* we live, and *what* we own) – our attempts at happiness will be as disappointing as a cardboard cake.

Oh, but the frosting is so good! As a kid, I remember getting to lick the frosting bowl after my mother had made a chocolate cake. I would use Mom's plastic flexible spatula, which would allow me to scrape the bowl absolutely clean. The first spatula full was great, the second spatula full was a bit sugary, and by the time I got to the third spatula full, I could hardly eat it! Can we live on only frosting and feel satisfied? I don't think so.

That was the turning point for me. When I finally got sick of the frosting and confronted the dissatisfaction in my life, I was driven to ask the one question that matters: WHY? Why do I live the way I do? Why do I do the work I do? Why do I spend money on the things I buy? To quit obsessing over who I am, how I live, and what I own requires asking the all-important question: WHY?

Why do I want a new car?

Why do I want a new job?

Why do I want a bigger house?

Why do I want a different spouse?

Asking this question makes all the difference. So, why don't we ask why? Because we don't want to deal with a question that makes us uncomfortable. Asking the why question makes us face the truth. It makes us gaze into our own hearts, which can be quite revealing. It's also hard work, because there are no easy answers. It forces us to move from thinking about the temporal to the eternal. It causes us to confront our origin, our identity, and our destiny. Satan doesn't want us to think about the why, because it risks exposing his deceptions. If he can keep us preoccupied with the who, what, and how, then he will never have to worry about us working with God to create great impact.

Asking why forces us to contemplate our purpose in Life.

Asking why forces us to contemplate our purpose in life. Our journey to a fulfilled life can't progress without it. I sincerely believe that a purposeful, contented, satisfied life can only be had by asking – and honestly answering – the BIG question in life: Why do I exist? Stated another way, what is my purpose in life?

So here is what I want you to do. Before you roll over and go to sleep or turn on the TV to watch your favorite team, before you hustle out the door to go shopping or to work, I want you to **STOP**! Find a quiet, secluded place and spend the next 20-30 minutes answering, in the most honest way possible, these two questions:

Am I satisfied with my life?

Do I really understand the purpose for my life?

After you have spent some time in contemplation, I want you to write down your answers. No, I'm not suggesting it will be easy, but it is crucial that you take the time to examine your life with sincere honesty. In the next chapter we will explore together the answer to that all-important question: *Why do I exist?*

END OF CHAPTER REFLECTION

Am I satisfied with my life?

_____

_____

_____

_____

_____

_____

_____

_____

Do I really understand the purpose for my life?

_____

_____

_____

_____

_____

_____

_____

_____

Everyday you must remind yourself of your purpose so that you do not squander away the opportunity of the day.

Luis Gutierrez

CHAPTER 2

IT'S ALL ABOUT HAVING THE RIGHT WHY

"It is not what a man does that determines whether his work is sacred or secular, it is why he does it."
A. W. Tozer

IN OUR LAST CHAPTER I ASKED YOU two very important questions: Are you satisfied with your life? Are you living with purpose? A logical follow up: Are you honestly satisfied with the impact you are having on the people around you, the community you live in, and the country you love? I also asked you to take some time and seriously consider your answers. I hope you contemplated this question about satisfaction, just as I did so many years ago. If you're like me, you may have concluded that deep down inside you know there could be more, maybe a lot more to the life you're living. And if you are not satisfied, then you must make a conscious decision to face the facts and make a change.

To make that change, I'm challenging you again to ask the BIG question: Why? Why do I live the way I live? Why do I work where I work? Why do I think the way I think? Why do I act the way I act? And finally, why do I exist? Or more pointedly, what is my purpose in life? I've come to realize that true change starts by asking and answering these questions.

As I asked myself these questions many years ago, it didn't take long for me to determine I was not fully satisfied; in fact, I was a long way from experiencing what I thought my life should be. I was growing weary of keeping up with what the world demanded of me regarding who I was, how I lived, and what I owned. The world was calling me to this self-centered purpose for living and trying to convince me it was success. I bought it for a while, but over time I determined that secular success was temporal, fleeting, and profoundly unsatisfying.

Each successful high was followed by an unsatisfied low, which led to a greater effort to have another more successful high, which led to yet an even greater unsatisfied low. The exhilaration of this year's profits lasted only until the end of the year when the quest for greater profits began anew. The next acquisition had to be bigger and better than the last. I was never satisfied. My pursuit of worldly success became an all-consuming monster with an insatiable appetite.

My pursuit of worldly success became an all-consuming monster with an insatiable appetite.

And not only was I dissatisfied with my secular life, it carried over into my Christian life as well.

I think as Christians the tension is even more pronounced because deep inside we really know there is a better way. We may try to rationalize our way into believing that life is just fine the way it is and spread a little Christian frosting in the form of feigned humility or self-serving generosity on our cardboard lives to make us think all is well, but inside we are still hollow and unfulfilled. Are you there? I was forced to acknowledge this realization by honestly and forthrightly facing the facts, the answers to my why questions.

In the process, I came to the point where I said enough is enough. I was sick and tired of the frosting. It was time for real change. I was ready for the first time in my life to confront those uncomfortable, philosophical questions I had always avoided. After a significant amount of late-night soul searching and counsel from my wife, great friends, and mentors, I began to seek answers for three classic questions of life: Who am I? How should I live? What should I do? Stated another way, those questions become: *What is my Purpose in life? What is my Passion? What should be my Platform?*

With this newfound framework for my life, I dug in to understand what the answers to those questions meant for me personally. God began to work in my spirit, slowly replacing my pursuit to live for me with a pursuit to live for something greater.

Now, you could be thinking, "I like living for myself and that's the way it's going be." Please hear my plea: it won't last, it won't satisfy, it will fail you one day and you will be back here wondering why life is so disappointing. I am convinced that this is a universal truth, whether you are a down-and-outer or an up-and-outer.

You're getting a lot of my story scattered throughout this book, but I'm not alone in facing disappointments that threaten to become dead ends. Listen to my friend Luis Gutierrez's story of wrestling with the big questions as a convicted felon serving a life sentence in federal prison.

Imagine someone taking your iPhone and disassembling all the parts, taking the chips, electrical pieces, and computer boards and placing them in a box. He then shakes the box so all the parts are jumbled and hands it back to you – along with the assignment to reassemble the phone by the end of the day. This is what it was like for me to figure out how to become a man. I was completely lost and confused, without purpose.

My entire understanding of what it looked like to be a man had come through my experience in gangs. Gangs taught me to respond to problems through violence and intimidation, a method that landed me in federal prison with a life sentence hanging over my head at the age of 16.

No one cared about me in prison. They exchanged my name for a number. I felt less than human. I worked several jobs, but they were just ways to pass the time. I didn't care much about anything, and I had no hope of ever getting out. Freedom was a dream that mocked me. Until my life changed more than I ever thought it could.

I got a job at Seat King and met Pete. Pete started showing me – while I had no sense of purpose – what it means to be a man. Life started making sense. For the first time, I began wanting good things for my life.

Working for a business that cared for more than just profit truly changed my life. I frequently tell people that when I started working I did not know how to read a tape measure. I couldn't look at the tape and tell whether something was three feet or five inches. But working for Pete ignited a hunger in me that has never stopped growing. A hunger to learn.

This hunger drove me to study late at night in my cell. It drove me to initiate a new friend group. I was inspired to learn more, to be more, to live a high-impact life, even when I had made every mistake I could make. Failure had characterized every aspect of my life. I'd ruined my record and messed up every prison I'd ever been in. But now I wanted to prove myself, at least enough for just one person to believe in me. No more excuses for failure.

I was more than inspired. I genuinely felt like a man for the first time in my life. My relationship with God was pouring a foundation for character. It wasn't enough now just to show up for work in the prison; I wanted to set new records within my job. Twenty pallets of seats might have been the best anyone before me had done, but I had a reason for doing better. The old records started falling, and by the end of my time there we had broken the old record by 40 pallets. I was no longer working for myself. My purpose had changed and my passions were evolving: I wanted God to have an impact on those around me.

Toward the end of my sentence, I started feeling out of place, like I didn't belong. I no longer had much in common with the other inmates. Something was stirring within me. The things Pete had taught me were taking effect. I would tell the guys, "No disrespect, but I am on a mission. I am going to get out, and once I do, I want to make an impact on those around me."

There was never a guarantee that I would get out. I remember being so disappointed after my first opportunity was denied. They said they didn't want to hear from me for another three years. But I didn't stop wanting to prove myself. I started going to classes, volunteering at classes, anything I could do to grow and improve.

I remember talking to Pete in the welding shop. He told me that if I really wanted something, I had to envision it in my life. So that's what I did. I started envisioning my freedom — walking away from the prison and what I would do on the outside. It changed my passions and helped me to accomplish everything I wanted within a year.

If you believe and stay faithful to your beliefs, God will make it happen. During my 23 years in prison, I found out how the internet worked. I could not believe it. This new passion connected directly to a new vision for my life. I constantly told myself that I was going to become a professional and use my platform to make an impact on people's lives. Now I am a week away from getting my professional license and my dream coming true.

Update: I now have a job where I spend an extended amount of time with people, giving me a huge platform for impact. I am always looking for how I can help someone in need. I love my job. I have met hundreds and hundreds of people now. I engage them with my life story, and I get to hear their life

HIGH IMPACT HABIT

Everyday you must remind yourself of your purpose so that you do not squander away the opportunity of the day.

stories. I am always looking for how my wounds and past can be used as instruments of healing for the kingdom. I am inspired by how much more I can do for others, more needs I can meet, more ways to be generous.

I always remember saying, "If they will let me out, that opportunity will not be squandered." The rest of my life is to prove that to be true.

Luis' story is nothing like mine. And yet the most important part is exactly like mine. Both of us had to learn from experience that appearances are often deceiving. It will happen to all of us who try to find satisfaction living for self. So, I urge you to stay the course with me. Let's discover together how to live the truly satisfied, high-impact life God created us to live. And that means living for something greater than yourself.

If we are going to live a high-impact life, we need to be able to love our *purpose*, live with *passion*, and leverage our *platform*. Our purpose, or the reason we exist, starts as a head thing, an intellectual pursuit of the truth. And as truth begins to impact our thinking, it also begins to move our hearts. We become passionate about the truth and it spills over into belief – head and heart combined. A full head and a full heart result in hands that live out our purpose and passions. Our platform begins to take shape. Let's look at these in more detail.

HOW THEN SHALL WE LIVE?

If we desire to live a high-impact life, we must ask ourselves, what does such a life look like? I believe it starts by figuring out how to love our purpose. In my pursuit of living for something greater than myself, my first step was to determine why I existed. At the end of the day, it is that pursuit that will lead us to the point of finding purpose in our lives. As I began to strip this deeply philosophical question down to the bare bones, I came to the stark realization that the competition is between only two possible answers. I am either living for myself or I am living for a cause greater than myself. And I believe those two options are mutually exclusive. You can't do both; you must choose one or the other.

> *I am either living for myself or I am living for a cause greater than myself.*

The great lie of our culture, even in the church, is that we can live part of our life for self and part of it for a higher purpose. We want to divide the world into sacred and secular, hoping to experience the best of both. But in the end, we miss out on the real life that comes only when we abandon one and pursue the other with everything we have. Let me explain this further.

If my purpose in life is to live for me, then I exist for the purpose of creating more pride, more pleasure, and more possessions. When my driving focus is on what pleases me, I will naturally develop a self-serving attitude and a life filled with pride. My pride answers the "How should I live?" question from its natural perspective: a passionate pursuit of self-gratification that will ultimately drive me to a life fixated on pleasure. Finally – and often the biggest stumbling block to finding our purpose – is our desire to own more stuff. Our self-esteem, our happiness, and our self-worth become entirely dependent on the possessions we own. So, if the purpose of my existence is to glorify *me*, then ultimately, I will become a person plagued with *pride*, enamored with pleasure and consumed by *possessions*.

LOVING OUR PURPOSE

But the good news is that there is a second option. I don't think most of us realize this, but we were made for glory. God created us as the final act, the masterpiece of His creation. Adam and Eve were created in God's image, magnificent and beautiful – until they began to live for themselves. They exchanged the glory of living for God for the glory of living for themselves. Genesis 3:5 reveals the temptation they fell for: to be *"like God."* And since that day, all of us have pursued our own glory instead of God's.

The turning point in my life came when I committed to living out the conviction that I was created for the purpose of bringing glory to God rather than to myself. That decision has provided me with the satisfaction and fulfillment I had been seeking. It was far beyond any secular success I had been able to achieve. Choosing to live for the eternal instead of the temporal, for something that is based on absolute Truth instead of man-made arguments, I began to live for my eulogy instead of my resume.

This meant focusing my life on the Creator, not the created. It moved me from a transactional life to a transformational life. In the end, it led me to the life I had always wanted: a life of freedom to love unconditionally, work diligently, live simply, risk abundantly, and give generously. And it all centered on making my purpose in life not about glorifying me but glorifying God. He IS the greater purpose for my life!

FELLOW TRAVELERS

My quest to pursue this newfound purpose led me to search out and find other men who had been on this journey before me – men who had already fought this fight. The blessing of having older, wiser men come alongside me was an essential part of my transformation.

As part of the process of being mentored by them, God was stirring my soul to discover something deeper, more meaningful, and much more satisfying. I developed a hunger for truth and spent many hours in God's word fleshing out what it said about my purpose in life. Through mentoring, prayer, studying God's word, and reflection, I finally came to understand the answer to the *why* question.

I finally came to understand that life isn't about secular success; it's about sacred surrender.

Let me ask you: if you are really living for something greater than yourself, then what is that greater thing? What could be so wonderful, so powerful, so satisfying, that you would give up living for yourself and pledge your wholehearted allegiance to living for it?

My answer came from my days as a child when my parents required us to memorize the Westminster Catechism. The first question in that great work is this: "What is man's chief end?" or in my words, *what is my purpose in life?*

The answer is found in the catechism question: "Man's chief end is to glorify God and enjoy Him forever." There it was, as plain as day – my answer, my purpose. My purpose in life is to glorify God! I finally came to understand that life isn't about secular success; it's about sacred surrender. Pursuing the former had left me disillusioned. Now it was time to go a new direction. Time to abandon my pursuit of pride, pleasure, and possessions. Time to begin seeking how I might honor God in all I do.

AW Tozer said, "It is not what a man does that determines whether his work is sacred or secular, it is why he does it." The result of a life purpose based on glorifying God and enjoying Him is a new life! *"Therefore, if anyone is in Christ, he is a new creation; the old has gone, the new has come!" (2 Corinthians 5:17, NIV 1984).*

Let's take a look at the updated Impact Framework below. You will see that on the left-hand side is my old life, the life of pursuing success with its purpose revolving around ME, as noted by the white triangle in the middle. This pursuit was accompanied by the passions (gray triangles) of pride, pleasure, and possessions.

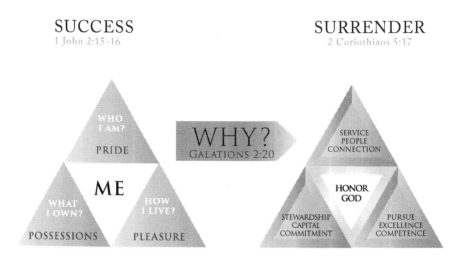

SUCCESS
1 John 2:15-16

WHY?
GALATIONS 2:20

SURRENDER
2 Corinthians 5:17

Personal transformation is represented by the right-facing arrow asking the WHY question. The move from success to surrender happens only when we embrace Paul's testimony in Galatians 2:20 to be "*crucified with Christ,*" no longer living for ourselves but living by faith in the Son of God who loved us and gave himself for us.

And finally, our new life, a surrendered life, is represented by the white triangle on the right denoting our purpose to live for Christ and our newfound passions of serving people, pursuing excellence, and stewarding capital. We have become "*a new creation*" and the "*old has gone*" as noted in 2 Corinthians 5:17.

This movement from the old life to the new life is represented by the white triangle in the middle of this diagram. It is at the center because everything else we will talk about in this book is built on the assumption that you are willing to make this transformation, or more accurately, that you are willing to let God change you! Galatians 2:20 says, *"I have been crucified with Christ and I no longer live, but Christ lives in me. The life I now live in the body, I live by faith in the Son of God, who loved me and gave himself for me."*

Only through the redeeming power of Jesus can we can die to our old selves and put on a new self. Through faith in Jesus Christ we can experience this radical transformation from a self-centered life to a God-centered life.

LIVING WITH PASSION

My understanding of why I existed drove me to ask the second most important question in life: how should I live? This *how* question is a matter of the heart. My new purpose required a change in my entire thought process. I soon came to understand that my passion for how I lived my life was about to go through a similar transformation.

Passion is a powerful thing. Look at the people you admire; their impact would not be nearly as great if they were not passionate people. Our *purpose* determines our *passion*, and our passion is that invisible force that allows us to develop a powerful platform. As my purpose changed from glorifying me to honoring God, my passion was transformed from living life with a set of principles focused on me (pride, pleasure, possessions) to a set of principles focused on others (service, excellence, stewardship). Let me explain.

Look at the triangles in our diagram. Let's start with Pride. In my old life, the focus on who I was resulted in pride. Now that I am living for something greater than myself, I have a new example to follow, and that's Jesus. God's word says, *"Even as the Son of Man came not to be served but to serve, and to give his life as a ransom for many" (Matthew 20:28, ESV).*

Jesus didn't come to earth to be a president, a CEO, a senior pastor, an Olympic athlete, an NBA all-star; he came to be a servant. And he came not only to serve but also to serve to the point of giving all he had, his life. When my purpose gets transformed, the object of my passion changes: my passion for selfish pride gets transformed into a passion for serving others.

Now look at pleasure. In my old life, my focus on how I lived resulted in the pursuit of pleasure. But with a transformed purpose my passion shifted from seeking pleasure for myself to pursuing excellence for the glory of God. My focus on a pleasure-filled life ultimately resulted in arrogance. I have learned that the difference between arrogance and excellence is motivation. Arrogance is driven by my motivation to glorify me. Excellence is driven by my motivation to glorify something greater, namely, the God who created me.

Finally, look at possessions. In my old life, I focused on accumulating as many material possessions as possible. I became consumed with what I owned. But with a transformed purpose and passion, I realized that God owns everything, including me. First Chronicles 29:11-12 says, *". . . Everything in the heavens and the earth is yours, O Lord, and this is your kingdom. We adore you as being in control of everything. Riches and honor come from you alone, and you are the ruler of all mankind; your hand controls power and might, and it is at your discretion that men are made great and given strength" (TLB).*

If God owns it all, then I must own nothing. With my new transformed purpose, my old passion for possessions changed to a passion for stewarding the assets that God has allowed me to manage.

A transformed purpose resulted in three newfound passions: serving people, pursuing excellence, and stewarding capital. The *why* and *how* questions were now answered, but one question remained: what should I do? What life decisions will allow me to live my life with purpose and passion? What occupation, profession, or career – or as I call it, platform – should I pursue so that I can live a high-impact life?

LEVERAGING OUR PLATFORM

If our purpose is a head thing and our passion is a heart thing, then our platform is a hands thing. Our platform is where the rubber meets the road. It's where we live out what we really believe to be true. And the difference between a mundane, dissatisfied, self-serving life and a high-impact life is the difference between merely talking the talk and actually walking the walk. This is why a platform based on a purpose and passion greater than yourself is so powerful.

I think in one sense God doesn't really care about what we do – whether we are a butcher, a baker, or a candlestick maker. But He *does* care *why* (purposefully) and *how* (passionately) we do it. Our platform should be a reflection of a purpose and passion that is squarely focused on honoring God.

In most cases our platform is determined by those special abilities and natural talents that make us who we are. You have been uniquely created for a special purpose. You have been given abilities and talents that will allow you to maximize your purpose and passion. As Psalm 139 puts it, you have been *"fearfully and wonderfully made."*

My life has taken a number of turns with regard to my platform. For most of my high school and college years I thought

I was going to be a dentist, but after taking a single business class I knew I was wired to be a businessman. We make our plans, but it is God who ultimately directs our steps. And those steps, if we will trust, obey, and follow His leading, ultimately lead us to a platform that is perfectly suited to who we are. When we have a purpose, a passion, and a platform aligned with living a life that is greater than ourselves, the result is deep satisfaction, contentment, and joy in the work God has called us to do. Our God-given talents, coupled with a transformed purpose and passion, allow us to maximize the effectiveness of our platform.

Unfortunately, we often make the mistake of questioning our platform when we are dissatisfied with our lives. We think a new job or position will be the key to finding happiness. Right after 9/11 occurred, our businesses went into a dramatic nosedive. Within a year, we had lost a considerable portion of the financial capital that we had created over the previous 20 years. Needless to say, I became very discouraged. My first inclination was to blame myself. I told myself that I must not be a very good businessman. I was also convinced that God must be calling me away from the platform of business and onto the platform of ministry.

As I began to work through the process of changing platforms, I realized that God did not want to change my platform; He wanted to transform my purpose and my passion and put my platform in a whole new light. For the first time in my life I could now see how to leverage my platform. What had become a mundane, unsatisfying routine turned into a vision that allowed me to be a part of living for something that was truly greater than myself. A clear vision of how I could live a high-impact life began to unfold.

This was a major revelation in my life: my platform was NOT my purpose; it was the venue, the career, the job that allowed me to live out my purpose, which is to honor God in all I do.

THE HIGH-IMPACT L-I-F-E

Let me unpack for you here what I have been referring to as the high-impact LIFE. I define it as a LIFE of stewardship. From this point forward I will capitalize the word to help us envision what a high-impact LIFE can be. Here's what I mean by the acrostic, L-I-F-E. The letters stand for: L – your Labor, I – your Influence, F – your Financial capital, and E – your Expertise. I believe these are the four assets God allows us to steward. From now on when I use the word LIFE, I want you to think of the four assets He has given you to manage: your Labor, your Influence, your Financial capital, and your Expertise. When stewarded properly, these assets provide your platform with unbelievable leverage.

This LIFE has high impact because it is transformational. It transforms my purpose from living for self to living for something greater. It transforms my passion from seeking pride, pleasure, and possessions for myself, to a passion for serving others, pursuing excellence, and stewarding capital. And it transforms my platform from a mundane job into an exciting, vision-driven, high-impact LIFE.

Here's the bottom line. Living a high-impact LIFE is the natural result of a LIFE of stewardship. If we have given up living for ourselves and have decided to live for the purpose of honoring God, then, by definition, we have given up the rights to all that we are, all that we do, and all that we have. We have given up ownership and have taken on the LIFE of a faithful steward.

If I view life as an owner, then I am back in the game of pursuing pride, pleasure, and possessions for myself. If I view myself as a steward, I am taking the assets God has allowed me to manage – primarily my time, talent, and treasure – with the intent of maximizing those for the single purpose of honoring God. And when I view my life through the lens of a faithful steward, my viewpoint radically changes. Life takes on new meaning and new purpose. Worldly success takes a back seat to living significantly for Jesus Christ.

THE FAITHFUL STEWARD

Early in this chapter I asked you to ask yourself, why do I exist? So, let's end this session with another *why* question: Why should I strive to live a high-impact LIFE? Why should I live a LIFE of a faithful steward?

I think the answer to this question is best summed up in the parable of the talents in Matthew 25:14-30. In the story, the master, or owner, prepared to go on a long journey. Before he left, he entrusted his wealth to three servants. While he was on the journey, two of the servants put the money to work and doubled its value. The remaining servant buried his portion in the ground and did nothing with it because he was afraid. When the owner returned, his response to the servants who had multiplied his wealth was this: *"Well done, good and faithful servant! You have been faithful with a few things; I will put you in charge of many things. Come and share your master's happiness!"*

But to the servant who buried the money, the owner said, *"Take the wealth from him and give it to the one who doubled it. . . . and throw that worthless servant out."* My paraphrase. There are three reasons this parable epitomizes the result of living a LIFE of a faithful steward.

First, God expects us to be good stewards and multiply the assets he has placed under our management. The master was not pleased with the servant who buried his talent in the ground. The lesson here is that we should not be afraid, as was the one servant; rather, we can risk abundantly if we are living for God. *"God did not give us a spirit of timidity, but a spirit of power, of love and of self-discipline" (2 Timothy 1:7, NIV 1984).*

Second, being a faithful steward will be the most rewarding thing we do. As the master said, *"You have been faithful with a few things; I will put you in charge of many things."* Wouldn't you like to be granted the opportunity to multiply your efforts and do more of what you really love to do?

And finally, we will live a satisfied life. Can you imagine standing before the Creator of the universe and having Him say, *"Well done, good and faithful servant?"* It just can't get any better than that. And then He finishes up by saying, *"Come and share your master's happiness!"* At the end of the day, we will be able to share in the joy and happiness that only God can provide, and it will be for eternity!

Let's look at our new Impact Framework and see if we can put all this in perspective. My Purpose, represented by the white triangle in the middle, is to Honor God. My Passion, represented by the three gray triangles is now to Serve People, Pursue Excellence, and Steward Capital. And my Platform, represented by the black outline of the triangle, is to now live a LIFE of a faithful steward.

IMPACT FRAMEWORK

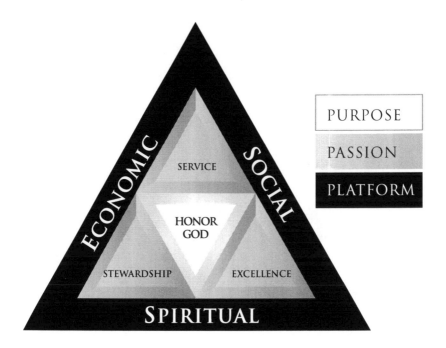

A high-impact LIFE, a LIFE as a steward, allows me to put God first, others second, and myself third. It's a LIFE that allows me to love unconditionally, work diligently, live simply, risk abundantly, and give generously. It is a LIFE filled with satisfaction, peace of mind, contentment, and joy regardless of my financial, social, or physical environment. And it is a direct result of loving my *Purpose, living with Passion, and leveraging my Platform.*

In the next chapter, we will dig into the important foundational concept of loving our Purpose and begin to understand how we can honor God in all we do.

END OF CHAPTER REFLECTION

Why should I strive to live a high-impact LIFE?

_____

_____

_____

_____

_____

_____

_____

Why should I live a LIFE of a faithful steward?

_____

_____

_____

_____

_____

_____

_____

_____

When God calls
you to a particular
journey, never give up
no matter how difficult
the beginning of the
journey may seem.

Cynthia Booth

CHAPTER 3

FINDING MY ULTIMATE PURPOSE

"Man's chief end is to glorify God and enjoy Him forever."
Westminister Catechism

IN THE LAST CHAPTER, WE UNPACKED the concept of living for "me" that resulted in a life focused on pride, pleasure, and possessions. We compared it to living for something greater, which refocused our lives on serving people, pursuing excellence, and stewarding capital. We discovered the key to making this monumental transformation is asking the *why* question. I challenged you to ask yourself, "Why do I exist? Is it to glorify myself or to glorify God?" From there we developed the idea that if we truly loved our purpose in life, which is to honor God, then a natural outcome would be to live with passion and leverage our platform.

In this chapter, we dive into the concept of loving our purpose; Honoring God. Honoring God is a result of wholeheartedly pursuing three key virtues. These are the virtues of truth, faith, and character. Before we get to these virtues, I want to make sure we understand how our purpose, our passion fit into the big picture of living a high-impact LIFE. So, let's go back to our Impact

Framework and look again at the relationship between our purpose, our passion. The white triangle represents our Purpose in life, the three gray triangles represent our new found passions in life.

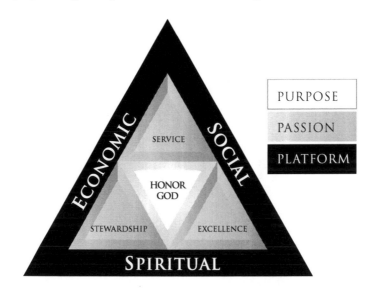

In John 15, Jesus lays out an explicit description for how we can live lives of great impact. He calls this bearing fruit. In verse 5, Jesus says, *"I am the vine; you are the branches. If a man remains in me and I in him, he will bear much fruit; apart from me you can do nothing"* *(NIV 1984).* If we desire to live a high-impact LIFE, a life that bears fruit, it starts with us remaining in the vine. Remaining in the vine represents a life that is absolutely, unequivocally committed to honoring God. Abiding in Christ brings an awareness that every minute we are walking arm in arm with God Himself. We have the assurance of who God is, and we know we are living our lives in accordance with His will and direction. The result is certainty: an all consuming, all knowing, all satisfying feeling that we are living a high-impact LIFE.

This is depicted in our graphic as the white center triangle, which represents our pursuit of honoring God. It is a symbol of the vine and our desire to remain in Him. It is the "being" part of our relationship with God. It reminds us that our inner transformation must come first if we desire to live lives that will impact the people around us. When we abide in Christ, we are transformed by the work of His Spirit that deepens our faith and allows each of us to go out into the world and "do" the will of the Father.

If the white triangle represents the vine or our "being", the gray triangles represent the branches of our "doing". These represent the three essential elements of "doing" in our Christian walk: namely, to serve people, pursue excellence, and steward capital. If our purpose is to honor God, then these three gray triangles represent our passions in life. James 1:22 says, *"Do not merely listen to the word, and so deceive yourselves. Do what is says."* This is how we demonstrate to the world that our faith is real and that our purpose is to truly honor God. We do this by passionately living lives of service, excellence, and stewardship.

Because of the Holy Spirit's work in our life, our old desires that were driven by our thirst for success are replaced by our new desire to surrender to God's call on our life. This results in three newfound principles: serving people, pursuing excellence, and stewarding capital. These connect directly to three crucial components of everyday life: relationships, the processes required of us, and the stuff we manage. Consequently, we serve *people*, complete *processes* with excellence, and steward all of the *property* entrusted to us.

Relationships of all kinds – family, friends, business, etc. – comprise an integral part of who we are and how we live. When we choose to serve them, we honor God. Mark 10:45 says, *"For even the Son of man did not come to be served, but to serve, and to give his life as a ransom for many."* Jesus is the greatest example of service. In fact,

He demonstrated the ultimate act of service: He gave His life for you and me. If we are to follow Him, we simply must serve others.

A second critical area in life are those routine, must-do daily deeds we call processes. Whether it's balancing our checkbook, going to the store, mowing the lawn, coaching our kids, or probably most important of all, doing our job, these should be done with excellence because it is through these everyday tasks that we demonstrate to the world our desire to honor God in all we do. Colossians 3:23 tells us, *"Whatever you do, work at it with all your heart, as working for the Lord, not for men" (NIV 1984).* Living a LIFE of excellence is not only what we should expect of ourselves if we desire to honor God; it's also what God expects of us.

Finally, there is property, all that physical stuff we own, from the socks in our drawer to our retirement accounts. It's critical for us to understand that the only way to honor God with all this stuff is to view ourselves as stewards and not owners. Luke 16:11 says, *"So if you have not been trustworthy in handling worldly wealth, who will trust you with true riches?"* We are just the managers seeking to steward these earthly physical possessions for the benefit of the Master.

All we do in life, whether dealing with people, carrying out our daily processes, or managing property, can fall under one of these essential principles of serving people, pursuing excellence or stewarding property. So, if our purpose in life is to honor God by remaining in Him, and our passion in life is to allow Him to remain in us so that we might be able to serve others, pursue excellence, and steward capital, the result will be a platform that bears much fruit. Our platform is our job or our vocation. It is a vehicle God uses for us to bear much fruit. And this fruit consists of the necessary physical provisions required of life, great relationships, and the understanding of how God, because of His love, came to provide eternal life for us.

In summary, a high-impact LIFE is the result of following four simple principles: *Honoring God, Serving People, Pursuing Excellence and Stewarding Capital.* You see, these four principles also happen to be the answers to four essential questions in LIFE.

Why do I exist? To honor God.

Who am I? A servant.

How should I live? With excellence.

What should I own? Nothing, because I view myself as a steward and not an owner.

The wonderful news is that there is great benefit in striving to live this type of radical, unselfish, transformational, high-impact LIFE. Listen to the words of John 15:11, "*I have told you this so that my joy may be in you and that your joy may be complete.*" Two amazing things happen when we live lives of stewardship. First, we discover that the God of the universe is joyful over how we live. "*That my [God's] joy may be in you.*" Imagine that. God is in heaven, smiling, excited and joyful over how you live! And the second benefit is that we are joyful: "*and that your joy may be complete.*" The dissatisfaction we had with chasing pride, pleasure, and possessions is gone. We now experience a joyful and satisfied life, at peace with people and at peace with ourselves. We have moved from living for the moment to living for eternity. We are now living for a cause greater than ourselves.

HONOR GOD

Now that we understand how our purpose, passion, and platform fit into the picture of a high-impact LIFE, we can go deeper to understand the essential attributes or virtues required for us to honor God. To do so, let's zero in on the white "Honor God" triangle.

To honor God is to keep his commandments. Jesus taught us, "*Love the Lord your God with all your heart and with all your soul and with all your mind.*" This is the first and greatest commandment. And the second is like it: "*Love your neighbor as yourself*" (Matthew 22:37-39). If we are to honor God, we must love Him with our head, our heart, and our hands. These are three distinct attributes of our being, and when all of them are working in concert with each other we are able to fulfill this commandment.

God has given us a mind, and we should use it to pursue truth. God has also given us a heart for the pursuit of faith. And God has given us a soul, which, when obedient to His Word, results in character. So if we are to really honor God, we need heads full of truth, hearts full of faith, and obedient hands employed with character. The pursuit of these three virtues – truth, faith, and character – are essential if we are to live high-impact lives and live out the principle of honoring God.

Romans 12:1-2 amplifies the importance of this trilogy. Paul exhorts us, "*Therefore I urge you, brethren, by the mercies of God, to present your bodies a living and holy sacrifice.*" That's living with character. He continues, "*acceptable to God, which is your spiritual service of worship*" (NASB). That's the exercise of faith.

He concludes with, "*Do not conform to the pattern of this world, but be transformed by the renewing of your mind. Then you will be able to test and approve what God's will is – his good, pleasing and perfect will.*" That's the pursuit of truth.

If we are to truly honor God, I believe it requires the spiritual disciplines of knowing the truth, exercising faith, and living with character. The reason many people are living mundane, unsatisfied, unfulfilled lives is that they don't truly understand the importance of these three virtues. Many people know the truth, some people believe the truth, but few people obey the truth. We have lots of head knowledge about the truth, but our faith is weak and ineffective and our attraction to the world keeps us from living high-impact lives of character. Honoring God requires intentionality.

Cynthia Booth is an inspiring example of knowing the truth, exercising faith, and living with character, as you'll see in her story of climbing the corporate ladder and then using those same virtues to launch an entrepreneurial career.

Originally I am from Cincinnati, Ohio, I am the oldest of three children. We were a modest family; our greatest wealth was in relationships with each other and with Jesus Christ. The greatest gift our parents ever gave us was introducing us to Christ at a very young age. I saw in their lives the demonstration of what loving Christ really meant: serving others and living our purpose with a sense of determination, tenacity, and wanting to see results in God's people.

I graduated a year early from high school and went to Denison

University, a small liberal arts school. Most of the students came from wealth and privilege, very different from my background. Fortunately, I never saw myself as being without privilege, just privileged in a different way. My plan was to finish college and go to the law school where I had been accepted. But with my undergraduate degree in hand, another plan showed up. I got engaged and decided to work for a bank for a year before starting law school.

US Bank changed the trajectory of my anticipated career path. My one year became fifteen, as I rose to unexpected levels at the bank.

In hindsight, it's easy for me to see God's hand in this. My plan was law school, but that was not His plan. His plan was to introduce me to the financial industry in which I would run six different company divisions, ultimately becoming president of a division. This was a life for which I had no previous exposure, but God allowed me to move through that company and reach a rank of leadership I would never have thought possible. He was equipping me for what He had ultimately destined for my life. I didn't realize it until I looked back and saw the fit for what I do today.

In 1999 I made the decision that after all the years at the bank there was still something missing. It wasn't that my compensation, the corporate life, and flying around on corporate jets weren't great, but something inside didn't feel complete. Without really understanding this, I just knew I needed to leave the bank. All I knew was that there was a calling on me. Convinced of the philosophy of "nothing ventured, nothing gained," I stepped out on faith to start my own business.

Unable to find a suitable small company to buy, I turned my attention to franchise opportunities. When I applied to become a McDonald's franchisee, they said they were looking for a certain type *of person. They reminded me that this would be a big change from a corporate job. "You will be working with a different kind of people. The people you will need to grow your business are nothing like the corporate types you are used to."*

They asked me to work in one of their restaurants so they could see me in action. I did, and the McDonald's team was amazed. "You are used to working with people who have PhDs or MBAs," they said, "but somehow you related in a remarkable way with people who don't even have high school diplomas. You really connected with them and they saw you as a role model."

This was when the lightbulb flashed for me. This was what God was calling me to do. It was never about selling hamburgers, fries, and cokes. It is about the people I could touch every day and influence on purpose, using my platform to live my passion, which is much more than my business.

McDonald's offered me the opportunity to buy a franchise, but with the recommendation that I hold onto my job at the bank and train at McDonald's at night, just in case I ended up hating the job. At that point I was in charge of 114 markets for the bank and traveling all across the country every day. I would get off the jet, put on my uniform and go work at McDonald's for 20-25 hours every week. This went on for two years! It was my opportunity to stay determined and walk in faith toward the Lord.

I kept my day job, kept my blue suit, but added a blue uniform. I worked at night learning the new business from beginning to end. I learned to understand the plight of our employees as well as the needs of our customers. I also learned that when you keep up a grueling scheduling like this, it begins to wear on you. Sometimes even a person of great faith begins to question the Lord. "Am I doing the right thing?

Have I made the right decision?"

I was always working the night shift, and I remember driving home at midnight with the rain so hard I could barely see. Suddenly I saw the flashing lights of a police officer in my rearview mirror. I stopped. He came to my window and asked if I was okay. "Yes," I said, "I just got done working a shift at McDonald's, and I am headed home."

"Make sure you buckle up and drive safe, because the weather is supposed to get worse."

At that moment I started to weep. I remember saying, "Lord, I don't know if I've done the right thing. I am really trying to decide if this is way too much for me."

My husband and I had two children. I was doing the best I could, but I was afraid I had made the wrong decision. "Please, God, give me a sign that I am on the right journey."

At that moment I remembered a verse that my parents had frequently quoted, "He [God] will never leave you nor forsake you" (Deuteronomy 31:6). It felt like my parents were saying it in my ear, right then and right there.

I said to the Lord, "I have come too far on this journey to think that you are going to leave me or forsake me. I am tired now and I have no clue how much more of this I can do, but I believe this is a task you have given me. I will keep running this race to see where it ends."

I started the car again and when I got home my husband was standing in the driveway waiting for me. I was still crying, and he said, "Are you going to be okay? Look, Cynthia, if this is too much, let it go."

"I can't let it go. I am on a journey and I have to see it all the way

through."

Within 60 days McDonald's called to report that I had mastered their requirements and more. I was now qualified to buy a restaurant. That good news, while welcome, raised the possibility of another major challenge: when McDonald's offers to sell you a restaurant, they may choose to relocate you anywhere in the country. Not at all what we wanted. But because of our heavy family involvement in the community, they offered to sell us one in Cincinnati, Ohio. Another sign to me that God was still near.

I put in my notice at the bank. They didn't understand why I would give up being a corporate executive and all the perks that come with it. When I tried to explain that I have a different calling on my life, they asked, "What does that mean?"

"I believe I am called to make decisions that affect people's lives beyond just their financial transactions."

They were not happy. "We'll have to think about whether we will accept your resignation."

We now own eight McDonald's. My son, an ordained minister, is in the business. We are so proud of what we do every day. We have the ability to touch people's lives, to change their trajectory, putting them on a path from Point A to Point B. What I am most proud of is that we can help our employees who haven't completed high school continue their studies and get their diploma. Some of them have gone on to college through our organization. It is an extremely fulfilling privilege to role model, coach, and work with them.

I remember an employee who was on assisted living and really struggling to figure life out. She graduated last semester from Indiana Wesleyan with honors and is now enrolling in a master's program. What a purpose! To be involved in people's lives, moving them from where they are to where God wants them to be.

Our job is not simply selling our product; it's changing the lives of our employees. When I look back over what it took me to get here, I say my journey was not easy, but it was so worth it! It's not where you start, but where you end and the journey of faith you take to get there.

The journey of faith Cynthia talked about (and lived) involved surrendering to truth and learning to live it out in her daily life. This road to a high-impact life begins with recognizing truth that is universal, unchanging, and eternal.

HIGH IMPACT HABIT

When God calls you to a particular journey, never give up no matter how difficult the beginning of the journey may seem.

WHAT IS TRUTH?

Webster's dictionary defines truth as, *"(1) Conformity to fact or reality, or (2) fidelity to a transcendent fundamental or spiritual reality."* If something is true, it is factual or real. Truth is fidelity to a standard. The starting point for determining if something is true is whether it is fact, whether it is real.

In our pursuit of truth, we understand that we live in a cosmos that is made up of two spheres; a physical sphere and a metaphysical sphere. Our physical sphere is made up of the universe we live in. It consists of everything from the very small – one of the 3.2 billion pairs of protein that make up the human genome – to the very large, the billions of galaxies swirling in space. It's as simple as the life-giving compound we call water that consists of two molecules of hydrogen and one molecule of oxygen, and as complex as an ever-expanding solar system with untold black holes and superclusters. And thankfully, for most of us, our physical world contains the so-called necessities of life: food, clothing, shelter, and maybe even some walking-around cash. Our physical world is amazing. It is miniscule, gigantic, baffling, and at times it seems mundane, but its very existence is miraculous. This is the physical world in which we live, and the pursuit of truth in the physical world is called science.

Our physical world is tangible, so we can touch it, see it, feel it, and examine it. The pursuit of physical truth often employs measuring, analyzing, or testing. When sufficient iterations of testing yield the same result, we conclude that something is factual or true. It is factual truth if it can be proved by established evidence. It moves from being a theory to being a law, such as the law of gravity or the law of thermodynamics. But in our metaphysical world, the pursuit of truth is not quite so easy. Meta is a Latin prefix meaning "after" or "beyond." So metaphysical simply means what is after or beyond our physical sphere. Our philosophy of life fits into this category, along with the pursuit of the answer to our most important questions: "Why do I exist?" and, "What is my purpose in life?"

In the physical world, we are dealing with factual truth, truth that can be proven through objective experimentation. But in the metaphysical world, truth is defined by its fidelity to a transcendent or spiritual standard that extends beyond our physical world. I would label this truth as *fidelity truth*. Fidelity truth is then proven real if it conforms to a certain moral standard. Defining fidelity truth requires that we first determine our transcendent fundamental spiritual standard.

This is not easy to discern, but it is essential because it determines the principles and ethics by which we live. It forms the basis for our moral code, which we use to determine what we believe to be right or wrong. Our answers to the questions such as: "Is there right and wrong? Is there good and evil? Is there love and hate? Is truth absolute?" are what distinguish humans from all other living creatures.

Our answers to those questions also determine the rules of how we live in societies as families, villages, states, or nations. This quest for fact and reality outside of our physical world, this fidelity truth, ultimately determines the relationship we have with God Himself. From that determination, we derive the answers to how we then live, including the principles, the definitions of right and wrong, and the moral code to which we submit.

Over the course of history, humanity has attempted to quantify and qualify fidelity truth. Great effort has been expended to determine the philosophy of life or the moral code by which we should live. Socrates and Plato pursued the meaning of truth. The Romans sought personal fortitude as a primary virtue. Medieval philosophy was greatly influenced by Christianity. Since the early nineteenth century, however, it could be argued that the pendulum has shifted and led us to the current idea that man, not God, determines morality and truth.

This shift can be seen by comparing the definition of "moral" in the 1828 version of Webster's dictionary with the most recent 2010 version. The 1828 version defines "moral" as, "Relating to the practice, manners or conduct of men as social beings in relation to each other, and with reference to right and wrong. The word *moral* is applicable to actions that are good or evil, virtuous or vicious, and has reference to the **law of God as the standard** by which their character is to be determined" (emphasis mine).

Webster's latest edition of the Learner's Dictionary makes a striking change, defining morality as, "(a): concerning or relating to what is right and wrong in human behavior; (b): based on what **you** think is right and good; (c): considered right and good **by most people**" (emphasis mine).

As you can see, the two Webster definitions are radically different. What was the "truth" in 1828 differs from today's "truth." In 1828, the standard for morality was "the law of God." Today's morality is "based on what you think is right and good: or considered right and good by most people." Truth has become relative, and I want us to see how this modern definition affects our answer to the question I asked in Chapter 1, "Why do I exist?" If I exist for me, to glorify myself, then my standard for determining what is true will be me. Truth will be as I desire it to be or as I define it to be. On the other hand, if I exist for something greater than myself, then my standard for determining what is true must come from a source greater than I am.

Our source for truth determines whether truth is absolute or relative. If we are the lord of our life and our purpose is to live for ourselves, truth can only be relative. If each person determines what is true, then everything can be true and nothing is true. We wind up with as many variations of truth as we have people.

But when we live for a greater cause and surrender to the ultimate authority, truth becomes absolute because it originates with and is determined by the ultimate truth giver. Everything else we will discuss in this book is based on faith in absolute truth that is rooted in something greater than ourselves: the ultimate designer, creator, and authority we find in the Bible.

WHY IS TRUTH IMPORTANT?

This is a pivotal point in our discussion, because honoring God is the most important pursuit of your life, and you can't honor the author of truth without striving to discover His truth. Truth is the foundation for every decision you make, and it will determine to what extent you can experience the high-impact LIFE.

Let me share with you my personal decision regarding truth. My basis for truth is the belief that God, the creator of the universe, has made truth known to us through His inspired and inerrant word, the Bible. Further, that we can have a personal relationship with Him through Jesus Christ, whom He sent to earth to atone for our willful choice to be our own god and ignore His protective direction. From this foundation flow the principles and virtues that lead us to a high-impact LIFE.

For this reason, I believe that truth is absolute and universal. I believe that God's word points us to the truth (John 17:17), that Jesus Christ *is* that truth (John 14:6), and the truth will set us free (John 8:32). If we don't get truth right, then nothing else is right. Faith in a lie will result in a lie. Without truth, faith is only wishful thinking, leaving us with no solid cause for hope. And who wants life without hope? Therefore, our number one job as we strive for the high-impact LIFE is to pursue the truth.

Therefore, our number one job as we strive for the high-impact LIFE is to pursue the truth.

Here are three specific reasons this pursuit is so important. First, it is the foundation for answering the all-important questions in life. It frames our worldview and gives us meaning. It helps us understand our purpose in LIFE and instructs us in how to live it. Andrei Sakharov, the scientist who developed the Russian atomic bomb, said of truth, "I've always thought that the most powerful weapon in the world was the atomic bomb and that's why I gave it to my people, but I've concluded that the most powerful weapon in the world is not the bomb, but it's the truth." Truth matters. It is foundational to everything in life.

Second, knowing Jesus Christ as the truth will set you free. John 8:32 says, *"Then you will know the truth, and the truth will set you free."* Early in my business career I came to an understanding of the importance of truth in my daily life. We had just completed the acquisition of a non-performing bank and were aggressively cleaning up the problems associated with several bad loans made by the previous owner. We were seeking to redeem the collateral of a large loan when the borrower countersued us for several million dollars. In keeping with common practices in the 1990s, we had highly leveraged this acquisition, leaving very little cash to defend the lawsuit. We started the process of depositions and quickly figured out that this was going to be a significant and possibly business-ending lawsuit. After four days of depositions and tens of thousands of dollars spent in legal fees with virtually no real progress made, I woke up on Friday morning in sheer panic. I realized that this lawsuit was going nowhere fast and the outcome was probably death by a thousand cuts.

During my time with God that morning I happened to be reading in Proverbs 6, which essentially says that if you've gotten yourself in a bad situation, go humble yourself and beg to get out of the situation. Really? Could that apply to us? Today? If this is God's truth, it is true for all time.

So at the end of depositions on Friday, I approached the man who was suing me and asked to meet with him. Amazingly, his attorney gave him permission to talk with me, so we agreed to meet on Sunday afternoon at his office. When I arrived, he greeted me with a scowl and pointed to a chair.

"What do you want to talk about?" he asked in a gruff voice. I got up from my chair and walked toward his desk. I don't know what kind of threat he may have felt in that moment, but it didn't last. I saw his eyes widen as I actually got down on my knees in front of him. "I am a follower of Jesus," I said, "and in my time with God on Friday morning I was reading in Proverbs. It said that if you are in a bad situation, go humble yourself and beg to be released from it."

I looked him straight in the eye. "This lawsuit is absolutely ruining my life. So following Scripture, I am humbling myself and begging you to let me out of this lawsuit."

He began to weep uncontrollably. I was totally shocked at what he said next. "I became a Christian two months ago. I knew this lawsuit was wrong, but I didn't know what to do about it." Within ten minutes we settled the whole thing.

Simple? Crazy simple. But I can still hardly believe I actually tried it. Taking God at His word in what seemed like an impossibly hopeless situation. You see, I finally came to understand the power of God's truth and the importance of applying it to my daily life. The truth will set you free. And aren't we all looking for freedom? Economic freedom? Social freedom? Spiritual freedom?

The third reason to pursue the truth is that Scripture promises it will guide and protect us through the everyday struggles of life. We are commanded to know the truth and handle it wisely (2 Timothy 2:15). Truth will preserve us (Psalm 40:11, NASB), guide us, (Psalm 43:3, NLT), and give us hope, (Psalm 119:43, ESV). The truth will bring us salvation (Ephesians 1:13), it will equip us to lead (Exodus 18:21, NASB), and it will allow us to know the difference between granting mercy and meting out justice (Psalm 85:10, TLB). The importance of knowing and acting on the truth can never be overstated.

HOW DO WE FIND TRUTH?

We know now what truth is and why it is important. So how do we obtain it? I believe there are four primary sources for obtaining truth. The first and most important source of truth is God's word. His inspired message to us should be our instruction manual for everyday living. The Scriptures are the revealed truth from God (Luke 21:33; John 17:17; 2 Timothy 3:16; Hebrews 4:12; 2 Peter 1:21) and the principal guide in helping us to understand both the natural world and the supernatural world (John 1:1-3; 2 Timothy 3:16-17). To find God's truth in His word:

We should *read* it daily. Joshua 1:8 says, *"Do not let this Book of the Law depart from your mouth; meditate on it day and night, so that you may be careful to do everything written in it. Then you will be prosperous and successful."*

We should *study* it. Paul instructed Timothy, *"Do your best to present yourself to God as one approved, a worker who does not need to be ashamed and who correctly handles the word of truth"* (1 Timothy 2:15).

We should *meditate* on it, as the Psalmist says in Psalm 119:97, "Oh how I love your law! I meditate on it all day long." We should memorize it, *"I have hidden your word in my heart that I might not sin against you"* (Psalm 119:11).

And we should *hear it preached.* Paul tells Timothy, *"Until I come, devote yourself to the public reading of Scripture, to preaching, and to teaching"* (1 Timothy 4:13). The pursuit of truth involves immersing ourselves in God's word.

The second place to obtain truth is through a personal relationship with Jesus Christ. In John 14:6, Jesus was asked by His disciples who He was. *"I am the way and the truth and the life. No one comes to the Father except through me."* (See also Philippians 2:5-11; Colossians 1:26-27; Hebrews 1:1-4; John 16:13).

A third place to obtain truth is through the *wise counsel* of fellow believers. Proverbs 15:22 says, *"Plans fail for lack of counsel, but with many advisers they succeed."* I have had two older mentors, both now in their nineties, who have walked with me through life for the last forty years. I have not made a major decision without asking them. I cannot tell you the number of times their wise counsel has kept me from problems and predicaments.

Finally, the fourth source of truth is God's revelation through His creation, our physical world. Romans 1:20 tells us, *"For since the creation of the world God's invisible qualities – his eternal power and divine nature – have been clearly seen, being understood from what has been made, so that people are without excuse."*

We have covered a lot of territory on this subject of truth. So let me ask you, are you pursuing truth? Do you know the truth? Do you want to be set free? It is the one thing that can give us true freedom. Sadly, according to the Barna Group's "State of the Bible 2014 Survey," two-thirds of Christians don't read God's word. Only one in ten are in a Bible study, only one in twenty-five memorize it, and yet 92 percent of people who read it on a regular basis say they feel they understand God's will for their lives. You simply cannot live a high-impact life without knowing and pursuing the truth.

FAITH

The pursuit of truth is the first virtue in honoring God. Faith follows. Truth is to know; it's a head thing. Faith is to believe; it's a heart thing.

What exactly is faith? Webster's dictionary defines faith as "(1) confidence or trust in a person or thing, (2) belief that is not based on material proof." In other words, it takes faith to live in the physical as well as in the metaphysical world. Faith, like trust, is based on what we believe to be true. Being confident of the truth allows faith to follow much more easily. This is why it is so essential that we pursue truth with single-minded devotion.

I think the ultimate definition of faith is found in Hebrews 11:1 (NIV 1984): "*Now faith is being* **sure** *of what we hope for and* **certain** *of what we do not see*" (emphasis mine). Faith is a belief so strong that it becomes part of our nature. Faith is stronger than knowledge. To know is to give intellectual assent. To have faith is to be inseparable from the object of your confidence.

Knowledge can be changed or lost by a more persuasive argument. True faith is so much a part of a person that it can be taken only by death. History has recorded countless episodes of the true faith of martyrs courageously dying for what they believed. We must add here a word of warning: faith, in and of itself is not necessarily good. Good results happen when faith is based on the truth, while faith in something false, evil, or untrue can be disastrous. How many people in Nazi Germany demonstrated faith in the lies perpetrated by Hitler? This was faith based on deception, and faith is no better than its object. The faith we want is placed in real, factual, fidelity truth. We can also understand faith by defining what it is not. The opposite of faith is fear. Dietrich Bonhoeffer tells us:

> *Fear fills us with loneliness, hopelessness, and desperation. It drives us to decisions and actions that undo us. How does fear do it? It hollows out our insides, until our resistance and strength are spent and we suddenly break down. Fear secretly gnaws and eats away at all the ties that bind a person to God and to others, and when in a time of need that person reaches for those ties and clings to them, they break and the individual sinks back into himself, helpless and despairing. Fear pollutes our thinking, distorts our judgment, cripples our resilience to evil, dislodges our love, and casts a gloom over our hearts. When fear dominates, then distrust, hatred, and selfishness separate us from our Creator and from our neighbor, replacing what unifies us: faith, trust, love. Fear takes away a person's humanity. This*

is not what the creature made by God looks like.

WHY IS FAITH IMPORTANT?

Faith is a living power that can move the mountains standing in the way of accomplishment. A person without faith is like a sports car without an engine. It may look fast and have a beautiful appearance, but it will get you nowhere. The stronger your faith, the farther and faster you will go. I encourage you to do a Bible word study on faith. You will be absolutely amazed at the benefits and the power of being a person of faith. Here are a few of them:

Faith is the key to salvation (Ephesians 2:8-9).

Faith is the key to healing and peace of mind (Mark 5:34).

Faith is required if you want to please God (Hebrews 11:6).

Faith is required for miracles (Matthew 13:58).

Faith is essential for a high-impact life (Mark 9:23; John 14:12).

Faith is essential for answered prayer (Mark 11:24).

Faith keeps you from being fearful (Luke 8:50).

Faith allows you to be righteous (Romans 3:22).

Faith allows you to experience and receive the promises of God (Romans 4:20-21).

Faith allows you to be strong and courageous (1 Corinthians 16:13).

Faith is a way to be blessed (Galatians 3:9).

Faith allows you to achieve your purpose in life (2 Thessalonians 1:11).

Faith allows you to endure suffering (2 Timothy 1:12).

Faith keeps you from being tossed around by the winds of doubt (James 1:6).

Faith empowers good works (James 2:26).

Faith makes your prayers powerful (James 5:15-16).

Faith enables you to stop living for yourself and live for something greater (Galatians 2:20).

Faith is the fuel that turns a low-impact, mundane life into a Christ-centered, high-impact LIFE of stewardship.

HOW DO WE LIVE A LIFE OF FAITH?

Exercising faith starts with the proposition that we can live a surrendered LIFE instead of a "successful" life. This initial vision – yet to be fulfilled – grows and becomes more solid as we exercise baby steps of faith, recognizing that God is at work in us for our growth and His glory. Our progressive journey to maturity takes a lifetime, frequently requiring us to wait and consciously choose to trust . . . again . . . and again . . .

Patient trust allows more glory to be reflected to God, because we are demonstrating faith in Him and not in ourselves. God-inspired visions always lead back to God. The depth and authenticity of our faith determines in part our ability to attain God's greater vision for our LIFE. Faith highlights our inadequacy and His adequacy. The bigger the vision, the more important it is that our faith be grounded in His ability and not ours. Often when we are walking by faith our expectation is that God will change our circumstances to suit us or to suit our vision. But His usual practice is to change us to fit His timing and circumstances – His greater vision.

A good example of this is when God declined Paul's request to remove a Satan-inflicted source of torment from his life. Paul's response should be our model. *"But he said to me, 'My grace is sufficient for you, for my power is made perfect in weakness.' Therefore I will boast all the more gladly about my weaknesses, so that Christ's power may rest on me. That is why, for Christ's sake, I delight in weaknesses, in insults, in hardships, in persecutions, in difficulties. For when I am weak, then I am strong"* (2 Corinthians 12:9-10). God's vision for Paul was far greater than whatever vision Paul had for himself. Make sure your vision is not just a good vision, but a God vision.

Exercising faith requires you to take a step. When God decides something needs to be done, He is looking for who will do it rather than how it will get done. He is looking for the person who will faithfully follow Him. I am often asked if I could help someone discern a decision they are struggling to make. I usually reply, "Are you planning to go but willing to stay or are you planning to stay but willing to go?" Don't sit in your chair expecting God to knock you off your chair as a sign to go. Get up and start going, and if you find the door locked, then return to your chair and pray, plan, and prepare some more. Once you have prayed, planned, and prepared, then get up and try another door. And if the door opens, walk through it. This is neither impulsive nor haphazard; note the emphasis on pray, plan, and prepare.

Faith that works is based on truth, and it requires you to know the truth. Investigate before you initiate. Spend time pursuing Jesus Christ, and your faith will grow. Determine to know all you can before moving ahead. God will often use this process to confirm or deny your direction. God's delays are not always God's denials. Investigation will further define and focus the vision. Let's be sure we don't let impatience, pride, or fear keep us from investigating what is true. Remember that spiritual ends do not justify carnal means. Don't move out in your own strength.

Faith that works requires more than compassion; it requires calling. Don't confuse your compassion to help meet needs with the calling that is required to live a LIFE of high impact. A life of faith is not a life of intermittent, feel-good highs that allow you to jump from one mountaintop experience to the next. Faith is a deep-seated commitment to pursue the vision and calling that God has burned into your soul. The journey may not be easy, but the rewards are eternal.

Exercising faith may result in a wilderness experience. Moses led Israel into the wilderness to change their superstitions and limited belief in God into a rock-solid faith. Your wilderness, whatever it may be, can accomplish the same for you. Embrace your difficulties as opportunities, and you will get to your promised land. Let the difficulties discourage you, and you will never accomplish your goals. My father would often say, "You can take the boy out of the country, but you can't take the country out of the boy." Moses had the same problem. He could lead Israel out of Egypt, but he could not take Egypt out of the Israelites. Only the difficulties of the wilderness could do that. The Israelites had been slaves in Egypt, and while slavery is the basest of human conditions, there is a perverse sense of security in slavery that is hard to wean away from. Even though the Israelites were freed and moving toward their destiny and fulfillment, every new challenge found them glossing over the terrible oppression of slavery and feeling that they had been better off in Egypt.

This is the dividing line that separates those who exercise faith and go on to victory from those who are faithless and go back to their old ways of failure. Until we make the decision that we will not go back and that we will be people of real faith, we will not go forward.

The most telltale symptom of faithlessness is grumbling and complaining. The one who complains has lost faith; he has already given up in his heart. The one with true faith sees even the biggest obstacles as opportunities to win a bigger victory and make a greater advance toward the goal. Real faith is not blind optimism that withers in the heat of the desert wilderness; true faith becomes stronger and more determined as the heat is turned up.

Exercising faith will require sacrifice. As we step out in faith, our journey will be like that of Elijah's. His concern was that the people of Israel were turning their backs on God. To stem this wayward tide, he built an altar, drenched it in water, and asked the Lord to consume the entire thing with fire. When the fire of the Lord fell on the altar and consumed it entirely, including the stones and water, the people fell prostrate and cried, "*The Lord – he is God!*" (1 Kings 18:39). Your journey of faith will require you to first prepare an altar of sacrifice and then wait on God to send forth His fire from heaven to ignite your work.

Exercising faith means having that faith put to the test. This happens in two ways; one is involuntary, the other is voluntary.

First, the involuntary. Because God loves us, He wants the best for us. And the best thing for us is to live a surrendered life, a life of great faith. God sometimes tests our faith in the process of helping us to live in total dependence on Him. James 1 tells us to consider it great joy when we encounter trials, because the testing of our faith develops perseverance, and perseverance must finish its work so that we may be mature and complete, not lacking anything. Isn't that what you want to be – mature and complete, not lacking anything? That's why we should embrace trials as a means of developing our faith. When something "bad" happens, embrace it. Ask God to show you what truth he wants you to understand so that you will be mature and complete.

The voluntary testing of our faith occurs when we consciously lay everything we have, all we steward, at the feet of God and say, "Lord, here is my LIFE; how can I serve You? Here is my labor, here is my influence, here is my financial capital, and here is my expertise; how can I use them to honor You?" We can only do this if we are people of true faith.

Faith that cannot be tested, whether voluntarily or involuntarily, cannot be trusted. Acting on your faith is the ultimate expression of devotion, admiration, and adoration. Acting in faith demonstrates you believe.

Faith that cannot be tested, whether voluntarily or involuntarily, cannot be trusted.

True faith is not a feeling; it is choosing to take God at His word. Matthew 17:20 says true faith can move mountains. It makes a way, not caving in to the thought that nothing can be done. True faith is true freedom; no shackle can be put on it. True faith is the ability to seize the vision of one's destiny with such a grip that it cannot be taken away until it is fulfilled. True faith is internal, not external, and it is not dependent on external circumstances. True faith does not diminish with disappointments; it becomes even stronger. True faith always turns the bitter waters of disappointment into the sweet waters of greater opportunity.

As we finish up this very important and powerful topic of faith, I challenge you to consider where you are in your faith walk. I believe that the best measure of our faithfulness is directly related to the quality and quantity of our prayer life. As I said in the section on truth, our pursuit of truth is measured by our hunger and thirst for God's word. Likewise, our pursuit of faith is measured by our hunger and thirst to spend time with the Creator of the universe on our knees in fervent prayer. This is not to suggest that prayer is the source of our faith; the source is God Himself revealed in His word. But our level of faith can be measured by the time we spend with God in prayer, because that is the behavioral indication that we are trusting Him for our direction and power. If we want our prayers to be effective, several characteristics must accompany them.

We must *ask*. God delights in giving to those who ask (Matthew 7:7-11). We must be *righteous* for our prayer to be effective (James 5:16-17). Our prayers must be *fervent*; we must really mean it (James 5:16, NKJV). They should be *specific* (Colossians 1:9-10). We should start with praise and end with petitions (Psalm 109). We must pray with faith, believing it will happen (James 1:5-7). And we should be purposeful, passionate, and persistent. Prayer changes things, especially the things that need it most – us. Prayer is a shield to the soul, a sacrifice to God, and a scourge for Satan.

Fervent prayer is hard work, spiritual warfare. In Colossians 4, Paul commends Epaphras for this: "*He is always wrestling in prayer for you, that you may stand firm in the will of God, mature and fully assured. I vouch for him that he is working hard for you*" (Colossians 4:12-13). This is no passive undertaking; it is an energized exercise of faith. And the result of active, fervent prayer is that we will "*stand firm in the will of God, mature and fully assured.*"

Faith is the assurance of things not seen. It is also the fuel that turns knowing the truth into living with character. Remember that our purpose in life is to honor God; we honor Him by feeding on His truth, believing it through faith, and living it out as we develop character. We cannot go from truth (a full head) to character (obedient hands) without great faith (a believing heart). A high-impact LIFE starts with the pursuit of truth, develops with a strong faith, and is lived out with great character. So let's talk next about character.

> *The one concern of the devil is to keep Christians from praying. He fears nothing from prayerless studies, prayerless work and prayerless religion. He laughs at our toil, mocks at our wisdom but trembles when we pray.*
> *– Samuel Chadwick*

CHARACTER

Talent is a gift; character is a choice. We can't all be NBA all-stars or world-class musicians or great orators, but every one of us can be a person of irrefutable character. Webster defines character as, "(1) the essential quality or the aggregate features and traits that form the individual nature of a person or thing, and (2) the moral or ethical qualities of honesty, courage, and integrity."

At the age of thirty I had just started my business. I had a two-year-old son and a daughter on the way. I had launched a small investment banking business and had left a good banking job – all because I had this burning desire to become an entrepreneur. It was exhilarating, and I was scared to death.

Having grown up on a farm, I knew firsthand the value of hard work and I threw myself into this venture with all the gusto I had. I literally worked twelve hours a day, seven days a week. The only other thing I did besides work was to spend a few hours every week with my family. My wife was unbelievably supportive, but after two years of this relentless grind without much to show for it financially, she sat me down and told me to get a real job.

After a bit of spirited debate, we finally settled on the plan that I would not work on Sunday and work only a half day on Saturday. This would at least allow me to have some quality time with her and the kids and provide me some needed rest. And guess what happened? Our venture took off and I had more business than I could handle. So what happened to cause this dramatic turnaround? Well, I – with the help of my wife – exercised this thing called character.

Character is the result of knowing the truth, believing the truth, and obeying the truth. It happens when we follow THE truth, Jesus Christ. I had known in my heart that I shouldn't be working on Sunday, because God tells us to honor the Sabbath. "*Six days you shall labor and do all your work, but the seventh day is a sabbath to the LORD your God. On it you shall not do any work*" (Exodus 20:9-10).

Unfortunately, I didn't really believe this to be true. Pride and fear snuffed out my flame of faith, and I thought the road to success was to work harder and longer. But when I came to the end of my rope and had to believe, God showed up in a very real and wonderful way. I went from merely knowing the truth that I shouldn't work on Sundays to really believing and obeying it. I exercised character. And when we become people of character, life is good. Peace, satisfaction, and joy crept back into my less "me-centered" life.

So how do we define character? I think it boils down to one word – trust. When you are a person of character, you will be trusted: trusted by God; trusted by your friends and colleagues; trusted because you know, believe, and obey the truth. God's primary prerequisite for service is trustworthiness. He is not looking for the most gifted, the most talented, the wealthiest, the most attractive, or the most popular. God is interested in bestowing His blessing on those who can be trusted. People follow those they trust. So, let your life and actions – not your words alone – prove you are trustworthy. Do more than what's expected. Keep your word and follow through. Pay attention to the little things. A person of character is a trustworthy person. A trustworthy person knows the truth, exercises faith, and lives a LIFE of character.

> *God is interested in bestowing His blessing on those who can be trusted.*

HOW DO WE BECOME PEOPLE OF CHARACTER?

Character is forged in the fires of life. It starts with truth, as the world questions our moral code. It then spills over to our faith, which the world also questions. And finally, our obedience will be tested. We will be asked to stand for what is right. God builds character into our lives by allowing us to experience trials and temptations.

Whenever we choose to respond to a situation in God's way

instead of following our natural inclination, we develop character. For this reason, God allows us to experience all kinds of character-building circumstances: loss, conflict, disappointment, difficulty, and temptation. To survive these tests, it is essential that we base everything on the truth, for when our faith is forged in it and further honed by obedience, the result is a person with impeccable, sterling character.

Character development always involves a choice. We will be tempted to do the exact opposite of the character quality we should exhibit. Will we choose character or will we choose compromise? The choice to base our life on the truth instead of our own inclination results in true character. When we make the right choice, our character grows more Christlike. This is someone who not only knows the truth, someone who not only believes the truth, but someone who has passed the test of *standing for and obeying* the truth.

> *Sow a thought and you reap an act; sow an act and you reap a habit; sow a habit and you reap a character; sow a character and you reap a destiny.*
> *– Samuel Smiles, Life and Labor*

To stand for and obey the truth takes supernatural power. We can't do it on our own. But we have access to that power through the Holy Spirit, who helps us in many ways.

He lives in us (1 Corinthians 6:19).

He helps us exalt Jesus (1 Corinthians 12:3).

He shows us our sin (John 16:8-11).

He guides us (Acts 8:29; Acts 13:2; Galatians 5:25).

He prompts us to worship (Ephesians 5:18-19).

He empowers us (1 Thessalonians 1:5).

He enables us to understand what is being taught in God's word (2 Timothy 3:16; John 14:26).

He speaks through us in times of need (Matthew 10:20).

He transforms our character (Galatians 5:22-23).

Character is revealed at the time of crisis or adversity when you have only one of two choices to make: Will I be a person of character or a person of compromise? Character is built in times of adversity; it is tested in times of prosperity. Without living lives of character, we cannot honor God.

SUMMARY

Let's conclude with a quick review. Our singular purpose in life should be to honor God. We do this by pursuing the truth, exercising faith, and living with character. Our pursuit of truth is measured by the time we spend with God the Father in His word. Our pursuit of faith is measured by our belief in the Son of God, Jesus Christ, and the time we spend communing with Him through prayer. Our pursuit of a character-driven life is measured by our obedience to God's word through the help of the Holy Spirit.

Faithful stewards honor God by pursuing truth, faith, and character. Let's take one more look at our Impact Framework. We started by understanding our purpose, our passion, and our platform in LIFE. And we have just finished digging deeper into our purpose in life, which is to honor God. We've seen how we honor God by pursuing truth, faith, and character. This represents the "being" part of a high-impact LIFE. In the next chapter, we will look at the first of three essential principles that should represent our "doing," our newfound passion in life.

END OF CHAPTER REFLECTION

How do you Honor God in all you do?

_____

_____

_____

_____

_____

_____

_____

_____

How would you describe your pursuit of Truth, Faith,

and Character?

_____

_____

_____

_____

_____

_____

_____

_____

Notes

_____

_____

_____

_____

_____

_____

_____

_____

_____

_____

_____

_____

_____

_____

_____

_____

_____

_____

Review your Purpose Statement every morning during your time of connecting with God. Starting every morning with devotion, prayer, and self-evaluation is the only way to grow personally.

Steve Reinemund

CHAPTER 4

THE GREATEST CALLING – SERVING PEOPLE

"For even the Son of Man did not come to be served, but to serve."

Apostle Mark

B Y NOW I HOPE THE VISION of a high-impact life is taking shape in your mind and beginning to stir your heart. I pray you are discovering your purpose, and what it means to live for something greater than yourself. I am excited to continue to unpack with you the four key principles of honoring God, serving people, pursuing excellence, and stewarding resources. In the previous chapter, we focused on the principle of honoring God by living out the virtues of truth, faith, and character. Over the next three chapters we will move from a focus on why we live – our purpose in life – to how we live, which is our passion in life.

I have come to appreciate the importance of rightly focused passion. If our purpose is to live for ourselves, our passion will be limited to our pride, our pleasure, and our possessions. But if we are living with a purpose to honor God, our passion takes on a far greater meaning. Our pursuit of success is replaced with a desire to be surrendered. Pride is transformed into a desire to serve others. The pleasure we once sought from extravagance is superseded by a focus on living with excellence for God. Our desire for possessions gives way to a passionate desire to steward all the resources God has graciously allowed us to manage.

Let's look now to the first of three essential principles that drive our passion for living: the principle of serving people.

SERVE PEOPLE

According to Jesus, the greatest calling on earth is to be a servant. Mark 10:45 says, *"For even Jesus did not come to be served, but to serve, and to give his life as a ransom for many."* Not only did Jesus serve others by providing for their earthly needs, He made the ultimate act of service by giving His life so that you and I could live forever. And if Jesus did this for us, then we are called to serve others: our families, our friends, our business associates, even people we don't really know. Think for a moment of the people who have served you. Isn't it true that if you had not been served by so many, you would not be where you are today? I think of my mom and dad and the sacrifice of money and time they made so I could be successful in life. I think of teachers and mentors who filled my head with knowledge and my heart with character. I think of the brave men and women in our armed forces who gave their lives for us so that we could live in a country that embodies economic, social, and spiritual freedom.

Service to others is the ultimate recognition of our desire to live for something greater than ourselves. It's the critical component that allows us to live out the second greatest commandment, "*Love your neighbor as yourself.*" Serving is the way we exemplify our faith, and it is the primary test of our devotion to follow Jesus. When we serve people, we connect with them on a deeper level that allows us to have meaningful relationships God can use to bring healing and transformation to them. And to us!

Since serving is such an important part of having impact, how do we serve people? The term can conjure up everything from performing menial tasks, to volunteering, to writing a check. Too often, we limit it to acts that assuage our guilt by throwing a bone of time to our favorite charity. But I think real service goes far deeper than performing a menial task or volunteering your time. It is much more than spending a few hours helping your favorite charity, and costlier than writing a check. Serving people as Jesus served will require the giving of your time, your talent, and probably your treasure. It's messy, it's dirty, it's emotional, it's time consuming – all the things we really don't want to do. True service requires making a relational commitment, what I call connecting. Most levels of serving are too shallow to effect real change because people don't want to make a relational commitment. They will give a few hours of their time or a few dollars of their treasure, but service for them remains a transaction, and the impact is usually low. Transformational impact requires connecting.

CONNECTING

I have found that this kind of transformational service requires the supernatural strength that God alone can provide. 1 Peter 4:11 says, " . . . *if anyone serves, they should do so with the strength God provides."* Serving isn't for sissies; it's hard work. But the impact you will have on your neighbor will be the most rewarding experience of your life.   Connection starts by establishing trust. Relationships that go deep and make a difference are built on trust. Genuine trust is required for one person to sharpen another, just as iron sharpens iron. Relationships involve conflict, emotional energy, time, and vulnerability. They only survive if they're built on trust.

Your marriage, your friendships, your business will thrive and flourish if you are able to connect in deep and meaningful ways, usually by serving. Here's the key: to serve at this level of impact means loving others as yourself. You can do this – you can love others – because you have chosen to live for something greater than yourself. Your purpose in life is to honor God; your first passion should be to serve others. It's easy to see this passion for service in the life of my friend Steve Reinemund, former CEO of PepsiCo. After learning it firsthand through the courageous service of his mom, he became a master at developing others while leading them in "impossible" missions.

I am not quite sure how she pulled it off. Mom, that is. As a single mom without a college degree, widowed at age 29 with three young children and never having worked before, I don't know how she did it. She is my hero. So much of who I am today is a result of the unconditional love she showered on us as she lived out her faith every day. She instilled biblical values into me that are reaping a harvest 60 years later.

I had always dreamed of going to a service academy. When I was eleven years old I wrote for my first college catalog from the Naval Academy. Eight years later my dream became a reality. Studying at the Naval Academy and then serving with the Marines was foundational to the rest of my life.

Through years of struggling to balance the many facets of life, I have realized the key is to keep the pendulum of life as close to the center as possible. Left unchecked, the wild swings will create havoc. The way I keep balanced is to constantly review my purpose. I keep it written on an index card that I carry in my pocket. I take it out, read it, and ask myself if what I am doing today is consistent with and supporting that purpose.

Over the changing chapters of my life, my purpose has adjusted slightly to serve each phase. Today with our children on their own, with grandchildren arriving, and no longer being in active management, my purpose statement reads like this:

"Love the Lord with all my heart, soul, and mind; seek His direction in my life and have the discipline to follow; live life with integrity. My primary focus is on the spiritual, physical, and vocational nurturing of my family, and on helping to level the playing field for others and leading them to a personal relationship with my God."

During my time in the Marine Corps, I met my wife, Gail. We have been married for 43 great years. I am grateful for her unconditional love and support through failures and success.

As a young Marine platoon commander, I learned the importance of leading by example. I also realized that what I really enjoyed doing was organizing a team, taking on tasks that people thought were unachievable and impossible, and figuring out how to unleash the power of the collective group of leaders to accomplish the task.

After serving in the military, I decided to get my MBA at the University of Virginia. Next was a job with Marriott International in a newly formed management development program. I started out as an hourly associate in a Roy Rogers Restaurant and worked my way up, passing through every position in the restaurant group until I reached CEO of the chain of over 500 restaurants.

In 1986, two years after joining PepsiCo, I became CEO of Pizza Hut (a division of PepsiCo). The industry was very competitive and innovative at the time, with several new competitors offering innovations including home delivery. We decided that we needed to enter the delivery business, but Dominos already had a huge head start. I assembled a talented team of people, all of whom were better than I was in their respective areas. After a costly failed effort, we developed a formula to win. In just two short years, the team introduced home delivery as a national distribution method and Pizza Hut became the leader in home delivery. Interestingly enough, every single member of that Pizza Hut team later went on to be a CEO or functional leader of a public company.

After my stint with Pizza Hut, I became President of Frito-Lay (another division of PepsiCo) and ultimately President/COO and then Chairman/CEO of Pepsico. I certainly never expected to be the head of PepsiCo; it was not my aspiration. I say that because it's important for people to take positions and work in places that they really enjoy what they're doing, not just to be prepared for the big job somewhere down the road.

After retiring from PepsiCo, I took the role of Dean of the Business School at Wake Forest, where I had the privilege of leading and developing future young leaders.

My career has really been shaped by my purpose and my passion for building successful teams and developing people. My goal has been to put together teams against a mission and empower them to develop and do their work in a way that is a win for everyone on the team.

When I look at what I have been able to accomplish during my professional career, I can honestly say that the best ideas were not mine; I was able to adopt them from others and assemble a team to execute them. My job was to create a principle-driven company led by talented and committed people who could recognize, perfect, and employ their God-given talents for the purpose of making each other, and the company, better. My life has had great meaning and fulfillment through knowing that my purpose is to honor God in all I do and my passion is to serve others.

HIGH IMPACT HABIT

High Impact Habit: Review your Purpose Statement every morning during your time of connecting with God. Starting every morning with devotion, prayer, and self-evaluation is the only way to grow personally.

I hope by now you see that the quality of the high-impact LIFE we desire is dependent on the depth of our ability to connect – first with God, as Steve's high-impact habit describes – and then with others. In my experience, there are several levels of connection.

LEVEL 1 CONNECTING – RANDOM ACTS OF KINDNESS

The first level of connection is what I call random acts of kindness. It's charity at its basic level. It's ringing the bell for the Salvation Army, volunteering to serve at the ticket booth at your kid's school, handing out water bottles on a hot day. It requires a little of your time and very little relational involvement. I don't want to sound critical of this level of connection; I believe it is a very important step in your journey to deeper service. It's a great starting point, but it is just a step.

LEVEL 2 CONNECTING – DIVINE ENCOUNTER

The second level of connection is a divine encounter. I challenge you to think of every encounter as an opportunity to serve. It may be brief in length, but think of ways in that short time that you can be an encouragement to the person you encounter. One of my favorite Old Testament passages is Isaiah 50:4, "*The Lord God has given Me the tongue of disciples, that I may know how to sustain the weary one with a word*" (NASB).

C.S. Lewis held that there are no ordinary people, "You have never met a mere mortal." A genuine interest in a person, an encouraging word, a thought for the day, or a sincere promise to pray can have great impact.

When my son went to camp, he was sought out by an older counselor who took a special interest in him. I will never forget my son coming home and telling me how spending an hour in the woods on a rock with an older person he trusted had a profound impact on his life. In that short hour, he was given a vision and challenged to think about his divine purpose in life.

LEVEL 3 CONNECTING – MENTORING

The third level of connecting is mentoring. It's the commitment by two individuals to journey together in a purposeful relationship.

A good deal of mentoring happens between an older, wiser, more experienced mentor and a younger, inexperienced mentee.

The primary example is a parent and a child. The parent nurtures, trains, and encourages their child to be the best they can be.

I was fortunate to have two older mentors in my life. I have not made a major decision over the last 40 years, either personal or business, where I did not get their consultation. And the rewards and benefits of this have been immeasurable. This type of mentoring provides you the perspective from one that has gone before you. As a result of listening to experienced counsel, you will make fewer mistakes.

I have also experienced the rewards of peer-to-peer mentoring or having a best friend. This happens when two individuals support each other based on similar life experiences. The primary benefit of this relationship is that it provides a real-time gut check on what you are doing. I have been richly blessed by having a best friend who has served me in this capacity for over 40 years. The encouragement and inspiration I have received from this brother cannot be put into words.

The last form of mentoring would be a younger mentor and an older mentee. You are probably wondering how in the world that would work. Once again, I have been blessed to have two younger mentors, one being my son, who have provided me a glimpse of life from a younger viewpoint. They provide a unique view of the future and a sense of hope, excitement, and expectation. While younger and less experienced, they have the drive, ambition, and perspective of a younger person that is so crucial if we are going to stay fresh and vibrant throughout our older years.

LEVEL 4 CONNECTING – DISCIPLING

The fourth and highest level of connecting is discipling. I believe this to be the ultimate tool for personal transformation. It's not only the most powerful tool but also the ultimate great commission for those who follow Christ. It's not an option; it's a command. *"Therefore go and make disciples of all nations . . ."* (Matthew 28). It happens when two or more people make a commitment, establish a plan, and agree to hold each other accountable for their personal growth and transformation. Discipleship is the process God uses for us to influence those relationships we have been given to steward. Through it we maximize the talents He has given us for achieving our calling. I call the person with this level of connection, this ability to disciple, a virtuous leader. A virtuous leader is a person who exerts great influence that is not based on position, power, or personality. It is derived from the authority received from God when living for something greater than self. Discipleship recognizes no social or economic boundaries. The custodian in the local school can have as much or more impact than the headmaster. The mailroom clerk can influence the morale of the company just as much as the president. The stay-at-home mom or dad can change the world by teaching their kids the importance of purpose, passion, and platform.

Virtuous leadership is the driving force that creates the ultimate form of serving our fellow man. And virtuous leaders bring three distinct virtues to the party; *Vision, Humility,* and *Courage.* They have the *vision* to see what *should* be done, the *humility* to believe that with the right help it *can* be done, and the *courage* to persevere until it *is* done. They engage the head with vision, the heart with belief, and the hands with courage.

The objective of virtuous leaders is to maximize the skills of their disciples, molding them into a team of highly capable participants who exhibit *Character, Competence, Commitment,* and *Connection.* They lead unified teams whose goal is to serve, to pursue excellence, and to be the best stewards of the resources they manage.

David was a great example of a virtuous leader. Psalm 78:72 says, "*So he shepherded them according to the integrity of his heart, and guided them with his skillful hands*" (NASB). David exhibited *character* (integrity of his heart), *connection* (guided them), *competence* (skillful hands), and *commitment* (shepherded them).

Let's turn now to these three virtues that are essential if we are to serve people as virtuous leaders; the vision to see what should be done, the humility to believe that it can be done, and the courage to persevere until it is done.

VISION

Webster defines vision as "the ability to think about or plan the future with imagination or wisdom." It's a mental image of what the future will or could be like. It is the ability to see the future with clarity and determine what should be done. Vision emanates from the mind: it's a head thing. It is the ability not only to see clearly into the future but also to ascertain what is good or bad, right or wrong about decisions that will affect the future. Expertise enables us to do things right; vision ensures that we are doing the right things.

Vision is critical to the high-impact LIFE. It allows you to see the possibility of great things and how to accomplish them. People follow vision because they are looking for something significant to which they can give their lives. Likewise, people follow virtuous leaders who can see and describe the future with clarity. Proverbs 29:18 tells us, *"Where there is no vision, the people perish"* (KJV). Without vision, you cannot live the high-impact LIFE.

I experienced a great example of how vision can serve people when we moved one of our businesses into a maximum-security prison. A few months into this grand experiment I became convicted that the inmates working for us were no different from you or me. They were just people who had made a great mistake. I realized that if God could redeem me in all my "me" centeredness, he could also redeem a criminal. So we devised a plan to help make redemption and rehabilitation a cornerstone of our workplace in the prison.

God had given us a vision to make this prison the most virtuous prison in the country. And the path to the most virtuous prison is to make sure it houses the most virtuous inmates. If virtuous leaders create virtuous organizations, then surely virtuous inmates could create virtuous prisons.

Could we help inmates who were repentant for their crimes embrace a vision for who they could be and the impact they could have? The first time I shared this idea with the inmates, they thought I was crazy. However, after working together for several years, they have seen our commitment to this vision, and many of them now believe in and embrace it. Great things are being accomplished by inmates who desire to be virtuous.

The importance of vision cannot be overstated; a great vision will allow you to achieve things you never would have thought possible. While a robust vision allows you to achieve amazing things, the greatest benefit of a vision is the impact it has on you as a leader. It changes you in a significant way. A God-given vision and its ensuing journey will grow your faith and character like nothing else. Great visions lead to great rewards, and having the privilege of humbly living out your life with a God-centered, God-inspired vision is one of the greatest blessings you will ever enjoy. A God-given, vibrant vision will magnify your *purpose*, ignite your *passion*, and leverage your *platform*.

THE SOURCE OF YOUR VISION

Now that we know what vision is and why it is important, let's consider its source and how we achieve it. There are two sources for a vision: human reason and the Spirit of God.

Visions born of human reason are not necessarily bad, but we must recognize the dangers in human-centered visions. Human-centered visions have created great good for the world: businesses built, diseases cured, the poor helped, new products created, etc. However, from that same source has also come great harm. World history is replete with war and genocide waged in the name of human visions of power, conquest, and domination.

We should also pay attention to the reasons that give rise to human-centered visions. Some are birthed because of a legitimate need or idea. William Booth birthed the Salvation Army to care for the "undesirables" in a polite Christian society. Today it is one of the largest providers to those in need around the world. Steve Jobs saw the power of microcomputers long before the rest of us knew what a microchip was.

Pride is another driver of human-centered visions. Whether for a new house, a bigger business, a larger church, to be the ruler of a country, or the desire to keep up with the Joneses, pride is a very motivating reason to dream.

Visions often come in response to resources that aren't being used adequately. "We have this vacant land, we have this empty building, we have this extra money in the bank, let's . . ." fill in the blank. And a vision is created to optimize the resource.

Finally, the most dangerous reason for the rise of human-centered visions is what I call the Visionary Leader Syndrome. Some people who define themselves as visionaries can't wait to cast a vision for you and everyone else. With all of their endless ideas, they don't seem to realize that a big idea is not necessarily a big vision.

A popular philosophy encourages us to make our organizations bigger and better by having a BHAG – **B**ig **H**airy **A**udacious **G**oal. In my experience, most BHAGers are not visionaries; they're just pie in the sky dreamers. They have all kinds of ideas but no concept of how to implement them. Someone once said, "Vision without action is a dream, and action without vision is nightmare." Whether for good reasons or bad, whether realistic or fantasy, human-centered visions are always limited by the frailty of those who cast them and those who are tasked to accomplish them.

God-given visions, on the other hand, have no such limitations. We quoted Proverbs 29:18 earlier: "*Where there is no vision, the people perish.*" A better translation reads, "*Where there is no revelation, people cast off restraint.*" The key difference between a God vision and a human vision is revelation. Vision is something we produce, while revelation is something we receive. Our magnamimus pursuit should be for a revelation from God Himself that can become our vision. If it is something He wants us to do, we can be confident of His guidance and provision. Living the high-impact LIFE places revelation before vision. Related to our discussion of human visions versus God-given visions is the concept of a *being* vision versus a *doing* vision. Remember our high impact model; we equated *being* with honoring God, and *doing* with serving, excellence, and stewardship. I believe each of us should have a *being* vision as well as a *doing* vision.

A high-impact LIFE requires a strong *being* vision. By this I mean a vision for the person God wants you to become in Him, the vision that will empower you to glorify and enjoy Him forever. Once you understand your *being* vision, your *doing* visions – or project visions – will begin to present themselves.

The *being* vision is about knowing God. *Doing* visions are a result of wanting to make Him known. The *being* vision is about developing a deep personal relationship with the Creator of the universe. *Doing* visions are about building high-impact businesses and ministries that create new products and methods for helping humankind, such as developing ways to eliminate poverty. I am absolutely convinced that your *doing* vision is wholly dependent on first having a *being* vision that will help you become the person God created you to be.

BIRTHING YOUR VISION

If your desire is to have a God-given vision for your LIFE, how is this kind of a vision birthed? In my experience, there are circumstances and experiences that come together in a Spirit-directed manner for a God-given vision.

A vision usually forms because of dissatisfaction or a desire to solve a problem; you are not satisfied with your life, you have a burden for the poor, you want to start your own business, you think that life would be better if there were a certain kind of widget. When I was forty, I realized I had become successful but not satisfied. The desire to solve this dilemma was the start of a vision.

Your initial dream may start with little conviction, but if it grows over time, greater conviction may turn it into a vision. Visions are usually championed by the person with the greatest conviction. I would add a caution here: make sure you understand the difference between the *why* and the *what* of a vision. Without understanding the why and only focusing on the what, you will probably not have the commitment to make the vision a reality over the long haul. Knowing and understanding the why of the vision will usually provide you with the much needed drive and energy required for its success.

Often during the birthing of this vision, you will come to a point I call the death of the vision. At some point, you will encounter enough obstacles that you will want to give up and let the vision die. If this happens, I believe it's because you are not ready to proceed with making the vision a reality. There is more preparatory work to do. In this situation, I encourage you to do several things.

First, **pray.** We often see only what we are looking at and miss what *could* be. Prayer keeps us looking for, and our hearts expecting, what we can't yet see. Don't just pray for miracles; pray for problems/opportunities that may come your way. Pray that you will recognize new opportunities that may be better ways for you to go. Pray that you will be able to see the process instead of only the desired result; you can't get to the end without seeing the way. Pray for great favor, as Nehemiah did. Pray for people, resources, and influence.

Second, work your **plan**, and make sure that it is thorough. Review your people, processes, and property requirements to ensure you haven't missed anything. It is also critical at this stage to seek additional counsel for insights and ideas that you may not have considered yet.

And then be **patient**. God is using your circumstances to refine your character, increase your competence, and test your commitment. Remember that God's timing is perfect. Waiting time is not wasted time; you are becoming who God wants you to be. God is using your circumstances to position and prepare you to accomplish the vision. Your present circumstances are part of the vision. God's work has purpose, so rely on Him to act at the proper time. Don't conclude that delays in achieving the vision mean you are not successful. Success is staying faithful to the process. If you measure success only by the achievement of your vision, you will face discouragement. Difficult time, painful time, frustrated time is not wasted time.

> *Waiting time is not wasted time; you are becoming who God wants you to be.*

Finally, take time to **ponder**. Make sure you seek discernment in every decision. Go back and focus on the *being* instead of the *doing*. As you take time to ponder, God will reveal new insights as to how you should proceed. God orchestrates what He originates.

A God-given vision will ultimately become reality. You will

always know the *what* before the *how*, so pray for the *how* to be revealed. Never forget that the most rewarding part of a vision is not how the vision will impact the world but how the vision will impact you. It is first about what God is doing in you. The vision in your head will become a passion in your heart and will result in a great work of your hands.

TESTING THE VISION

Now that we have a vision, how do we know it is real? How can we confirm that it is from God? I encourage you to consider several tests to make sure your vision is real.

The first is a test of **motive**. We must ask ourselves, "Am I pursuing this vision because I am doing it for myself or for something greater than myself?" A vision done for myself is usually a good vision instead of a God vision, and it will never have the impact of a God vision. Motive is also confirmed by the fact that you may try to give the vision away or discount it, but it continues to come back as a strong pull on your heart. You will have a moral imperative to make it a reality. I also think you will often develop a clear, vivid image of what needs to be done.

A second test is **alignment**. Does the vision align with God's Word? Does it align with human law? If you are the champion of the vision, does it align with your capabilities? Does it align with your experience, passions, personality, and spiritual gifts? Does it align with what God is doing in the world? Will it make a significant difference for eternity?

A third test is **resources**. God's work will never lack God's resources. We were involved in starting a Christian high school many years ago. We had been planning this project for over two years. God worked in miraculous ways during this two-year period. He had provided a $500,000 piece of land as an answer for us to move forward. He had provided a $500,000 cash contribution to confirm our vision. He had provided a great faculty and a free space to begin. But just sixty days before we were to open the doors, we had only eight students. Despite all the resources God had provided to this point, we still questioned Him. Once again, we sought counsel, we prayed, we planned, we were patient, and we pondered. Two things happened during this time. We were compelled to take aggressive action to market the school. I think this was important because it forced us to publicly display our faith. Second, God gave us the idea to start with an eighth-grade class and not a senior class. What senior would come to a brand new school? But we had many interested eighth graders. Two months later we opened the doors of the school with 61 students.

In a few years the school had grown to 180 students and we had outgrown our temporary facilities. Two years of raising funds yielded only $300,000 in pledges. We were discouraged and wanted to give up but once again we prayed, we planned (even more), we were patient, we pondered (with wise counselors), and soon thereafter God provided $3 million to build the building. God will provide for whatever He starts.

Another essential test is the test of **time**. Too often we become excited about the vision and we want to rush out and make it happen. We begin to exert human effort instead of waiting for God to work. This is closely related to the test of resources. I have seen people rush out and borrow money for a project instead of waiting for God to provide. This usually results in future problems.

Most visions do not require immediate action. One of the greatest benefits to waiting is that it matures the vision. You begin to see more detail and can short-circuit potential problems. By waiting, God is also maturing you. Your vision is merely an extension of what God wants to accomplish, so make sure you have fully vetted how it relates to His priorities. There is usually a correlation between the waiting time and the magnitude of the task to which we are called, which means the vision will likely increase in size with the amount of time you spend seeking God's direction.

The last and perhaps most difficult test is your willingness to **surrender** on behalf of the vision. The vision is not about you or your success. It's not even about your satisfaction with life. It's about your surrender to the creator of the universe, surrender to the point of where you are nothing and He is everything.

Surrender usually means personal sacrifice. The decision to personally sacrifice is crucial to whether your vision will succeed or fail, because it signifies your willingness to walk solely by faith. Throughout history, God has chosen to use those who are surrendered to accomplish great things. He views our sacrifices as worship.

These sacrifices are both spiritual and physical. God often uses physical sacrifice to pave the way for spiritual renewal. Sacrifice seals your commitment, causing your idea to become a passion. Physical sacrifice serves as an invitation for divine intervention. Having crossed the line of sacrifice, you have cast your lot with the heavenly Father in a tangible way and have become increasingly dependent on Him. Sacrifice may come in the form of attacks on your character. Soon after Nehemiah cemented the vision that he should rebuild the walls of his home town of Jerusalem, he experienced mocking, ridicule, anger, attacks, deceit, slander, and trickery. Surrender does not happen without personal sacrifice.

SHARING THE VISION

Now that we have a God-given vision and have confirmed that it is real, what do we do next? For a vision to have impact and make a difference, it must be communicated to the people whom it will affect. Effectively communicating your God-given vision involves several key factors.

The first factor is timing. Don't broadcast the vision too soon. Make sure you have gone through all the steps of confirming that it is real. You must know the why before you communicate the *what* of the vision. You must understand not only what it *could* be but also what it *should* be. The why will make the vision understandable, which is essential if people are to believe in it.

The second factor is selecting your audience. Begin by casting the vision to a smaller select group of people you trust. Then listen to their response. This will help you define and refine it. If they buy in, it is a good signal that the vision is worthwhile.

How you communicate the vision is also critical to its success. You must communicate and show how this is a God-given vision and not merely a human vision. People are looking to give their life to something bigger than themselves. It's not about you; it's about something bigger than you. For a vision to move people, the people must believe that it is a promise from Almighty God and not just the dream of an ambitious leader.

Even with a God-given vision, however, your role as a leader is still vitally important. You must clearly define the problem, propose a solution that engages the imagination, and give people a compelling reason why it must be done – one that will not only engage their mind but their heart. People will give what they feel they can afford to meet a need, but they will give sacrificially toward a vision that bears the marks of God's involvement. State it clearly, show it creatively, repeat it constantly. Explain it with stories and symbols. Habakkuk 2:2 says, "*Write the vision and engrave it plainly on tablets so that the one who reads it may run*" (AMP).

A critical reason why vision is so important is that it creates hope. Hope is the sense of confidence that what I desire can be attained. It is the sense that vision can become reality. Vision is a head thing; hope is a heart thing. It's the precursor to faith. Hebrews 11:1 says, "*Now faith is being sure of what we hope for and certain of what we do not see*" (NIV 1984).

Earlier I shared how we had cast a vision for the inmates who work for us. We told them we wanted to have the best prison in the United States. I remember that day vividly, because when I cast that vision to them, they laughed out loud. After all, aren't "best prison" and "virtuous inmates" oxymorons? Slowly, however, as we began to keep our word, to lead, to take concrete action, to constantly recast the vision, and to demonstrate that we cared about them as persons, doubters became believers. In a prison without hope, hope began to flourish.

I was never a runner, but in high school I decided to go out for cross country. I had an ulterior motive. And no, it was not a girl: I loved basketball. One day the high school basketball coach let me in on a little secret. "Pete, if you want to play for me, you need to run cross country. I want you in top shape when the basketball season starts."

That was all I needed to hear. Cross country, here I come. I will never forget our first meet that season. I had never seen a race with 250 contestants. But here we were – all of us eager hopefuls lined up with muscles straining to take off and prove our worth. We waited. And waited some more as the line was adjusted and last-minute details attended to.

Then suddenly, *crack*! The gun startled me. Everyone around me raced forward and I instinctively moved along with them. At first it was like a herd of wild horses jockeying for position. After what seemed like a long time and miles of ground covered, I realized I wasn't that far behind the lead runners. And what's more, I felt good!

Hope began to well up in me. I started believing that I could win this race. My lackadaisical attitude of just going through the motions for training now became a vision of actually winning. Hope replaced hopelessness, and my stride began to quicken. With about 25 runners ahead of me I could vaguely make out the finish line in the distance. If I wanted to win – or at least place – it was time to make my move. I kicked it into high gear, surprised and pleased that I had that much energy for my final sprint to the finish line. I passed one runner, then another, and another. This was exhilarating! Before I knew it I was in fifth place and still gaining. I fastened my gaze on my immediate target, the front runner, and strained to catch him.

Suddenly, with the finish gates in sight, he took a hard-left turn and kept on running. *What in the world is he doing?* I wondered. Fifty yards later the realization hit me: we had only finished the first lap. There was a second lap to go!

My hopes crashed. My energy vanished. I had to adjust to a new and painful reality. I'm proud to say I finished the race, but not in the top 5. Or 25. Or even the top half. I finished at number 157. No glory that day. The student reporters and cameras had already left. But I learned an extremely important lesson about the power of hope.

Hope can pull us into accomplishing great things. And its loss can make life miserable. People who have overcome great odds or survived tragedies and life-threatening circumstances frequently talk about the importance of hope and how it enabled them to survive. And without a vision, hope is difficult, if not impossible, to create. Hope is the driving force that takes a vision and starts to make it a reality. It's that deep-down feeling, that spark that makes us begin to believe.

Hope works in our physical world as well as in our metaphysical world. Hope provides that bit of assurance that we can recover from a health problem or get a new product launched. Spiritually, it's the confidence that we will live eternally because of God's Spirit living in us. Romans 15:13 says *"May the God of hope fill you with all joy and peace as you trust in him, so that you may overflow with hope by the power of the Holy Spirit"* (NIV 1984).

Hope. It's that intangible conviction that makes a vision a reality. It is created by an authentic leader gifted with the ability to connect. It is attained by authentic, trusted leaders serving people by casting a great vision. To have vision is to see what *should* be done, and to have hope is to believe it *can* be done.

Vision is the end, the finish line, but we start with it because success is most easily achieved when you start with the end in mind. It helps us determine and articulate the intermediate goals we need to achieve. It allows us to see not only where we are but where we are going, and it does it with great clarity. But vision alone, vision without humility and courage, will not achieve great things. That brings us to the second virtue, humility.

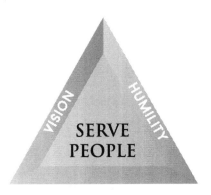

HUMILITY

It doesn't matter where we look, whether in business, politics, sports, or entertainment, it is absolutely clear that we live in a world of self-celebration. We live in a world focused on ME. Self-aggrandizing has become the norm. Self-confidence is being promoted at every turn as the way to a successful and satisfying life. And unfortunately, bluster and hubris are mistaken for ability and effectiveness. This disconnect from reality results in vigorous chest beating by those who vastly overestimate their capabilities and impact. Pride rules the day.

The opposite of pride is humility. Humility involves accurately assessing our strengths and weaknesses and seeing them in the context of the larger whole. It occurs when, through faith, we come to the realization that our purpose in life is not to glorify ourselves but to live for something far greater. Humility means putting God and others ahead of our own self-interests. We all have had the privilege of being around truly humble people. They lead quietly, modestly, but with so much inner strength and resolve that those around them cannot help but be inspired and challenged to loyal service.

Let's take a deeper look at humility. It is not necessarily great hospitality, or a kind and courteous demeanor. It has nothing to do with being weak, meek, or indecisive. Humble people don't necessarily shun publicity. They don't describe themselves as humble, and they are not embarrassed, humiliated or ashamed. Instead, they are secure in their identity and live with great purpose and passion.

WHY BE HUMBLE?

First, as Christ followers, it is commanded. *"For everyone who exalts himself will be humbled, and he who humbles himself will be exalted"* (Luke 14:11). *"Be completely humble and gentle; be patient, bearing with one another in love"* (Ephesians 4:2). As usual, God's commands reward obedience. If you want to be lifted up, then be humble. *"Humble yourselves before the Lord, and he will lift you up"* (James 4:10).

To avoid troubles, exercise humility. *"Remember how the Lord your God led you all the way in the desert these forty years, to humble you and to test you in order to know what was in your heart, whether or not you would keep his commands"* (Deuteronomy 8:2). Psalms 25:9 adds, *"He guides the humble in what is right and teaches them his way."* Additionally, the benefits of humility in business are surprisingly documented. A Journal of Management study found that humble CEOs were often characterized by three policies they implemented within their organizations: (1) reduced pay disparity, (2) high innovation and diversity, and (3) dispersed power. They consequently had lower employee turnover, higher employee satisfaction, and better company financial performance.

Researchers Bradley Owens and David Hekman have done extensive research on humility in leaders. Their expansive studies have included leaders from the military to manufacturing to ministry. Through interviews, field research and lab experiments, they've concluded that the hallmark of a humble leader is his willingness to admit his mistakes and limitations. They noted that successful military officers are egalitarian when planning but authoritarian in the midst of a dangerous mission requiring command leadership. Subordinates usually rise to higher levels when led by a humble leader.

Additional instructive conclusions from the study: because humble leaders don't believe that success is inevitable, they constantly test their progress, revise plans, and solicit feedback. Humble leaders encourage subordinates to take initiative, and they celebrate the accomplishments of others over their own.

HOW DO I BECOME A HUMBLE SERVANT?

Since humility is the honest assessment of our strengths and weaknesses, is commanded by God, is a key to truly serving others, and ultimately yields better results in our leadership, then how do we become humble people?

Humility is a result of obeying the first and second great commandments; *"Love the Lord your God with all your heart and with all your soul and with all your mind . . . Love your neighbor as yourself"* (Matthew 22:37-39). True humility can only be attained by the authentic transformation of our purpose in life from living for self to living for something greater. In other words, surrendering to the lordship of Jesus Christ, which then transforms our hearts and minds to a purpose that allows us to truly honor God in all we do.

Humility cannot be attained by our own fleshly efforts; the very attempt promotes pride. Humility happens when we acknowledge that Christ in us must increase and we must decrease. Here are a few very practical suggestions to help you improve your serving with humility.

1. Understand that you are NOT God. You may be extremely bright and talented but you are not the creator of the universe. There is always someone out there better than you. Rely on them,

defer to them, and delegate to them when appropriate.

2. Subject yourself to a 360 review. Anonymous feedback from the people who surround you may constitute a mirror you won't enjoy gazing into, but as Ann Landers wrote: "Don't accept your dog's admiration as conclusive evidence that you are wonderful."

3. Ditch the self-promotional aggrandizement. At every turn sincerely compliment and rely on those whom you are called to serve. Be sure to share your own struggles, failures, and lessons.

4. Embrace a spirit of service. Employees are quick to determine authentic leaders who really care and are there to help them out. Both employees and customers intuitively discern who is looking out for their welfare versus who is merely self-serving.

Humility coupled with great vision creates an atmosphere where significant things can be accomplished. Unfortunately, life does not always go as planned. Here is where the last virtue, courage, is required.

COURAGE

Courage is the mental or moral strength to venture into and persevere in danger, fear, or difficulty. It's the ability to do what is right or even what seems impossible in times of great trial. Courage is not a spur of the moment impulsive action but a predetermined choice to live by a certain standard. The word "courage" stems from the Latin word "cor," which means heart. Courage can only happen with a faithful heart.   Courage has been at the core of many of the great accomplishments we have seen in history. Courage allowed the United States of America to stand for racial equality and to survive a brutal civil war, even at the cost of 600,000 casualties. Courage allowed America to defeat the scourges of Nazism, communism, fascism, and terrorism. Courage propelled the founders of the United States of America to declare that "for the support of this Declaration, with a firm reliance on the protection of Divine Providence, we mutually pledge to each other, our Lives, our Fortunes, and our sacred Honor." And many of those founders lost both their lives and their fortunes. The greatest example of courage culminated in Christ dying a horrible death so that you and I could spend eternity in heaven.

The importance of courage is essential if we are going to live a high-impact LIFE. Without courage, we will never start our business, reach out to a person we don't know, leave a high-paying job to serve the poor and needy, change careers, speak up for the underdog, make a lifelong commitment, or stand up for what we believe to be morally true. Courage is what separates dreamers from doers. Courage is crucial for a virtuous LIFE. C.S. Lewis once said, "Courage is the form of every virtue at its testing point." Courage is essential if we are to retain a moral imperative based on our Judeo-Christian values. Recent days have shown headlines and media images of Christians around the world suffering because of their faith. Will we remain courageous in the face of persecution?

Courage is also commanded. Moses had led the Israelites out of slavery in Egypt and was leading them to the Promised Land. But because of their disobedience and lack of faith, they were forced to wander in the desert for 40 years. None of the original group, including Moses, was allowed to enter the Promised Land except for two leaders, Joshua and Caleb. As they were entering the Promised Land, God told Joshua, *"Have I not commanded you? Be strong and courageous"* (Joshua 1:9). Joshua was taking over as commander and chief from the great leader Moses and additionally had the task of conquering a new land with formidable enemies. And what was God's command? *"Be strong and courageous."*

FINDING COURAGE

Courage is the result of conviction, and conviction happens when your head is filled with truth and your heart, with faith. Once you have become convicted with your head and believe with your heart, the courage to put your hands to the task follows.

1 Corinthians 16:13 says, *"Be on your guard; stand firm in the faith; be courageous; be strong."* The first thing we must do is to be on our guard. In other words, relentlessly pursue the truth, be shrewd, and investigate; operate with a full head.

Second, we are to stand firm in the faith. With a firm, unwavering conviction, believe the truth! Operate with a full heart. This then allows us to be strong and courageous. A full head coupled with a faithful heart results in great conviction, which creates commitment and is followed by courage. Courage is the result of a strong commitment to live for something greater than yourself.

The reason for courageous action is not to be a hero, to fulfill a lust for adventure, to become a self-made person, or even to fulfill a desire to earn God's blessing. Courage is not the result of some pumped up, emotionally driven, spur of the moment quest to conquer the latest problem.

Courage is the result of prayer, planning, and preparation. The real reason for courageous action is to see our faith put to the test so that ultimately we may honor God in an ever-increasing, faith-filled way. Many people know the truth, and some people believe the truth, but there are very few people who have the courageous conviction to live it out.

Courage is also easier if you are part of a team. Ecclesiastes 4:12 tells us that one may be overpowered but two can defend themselves. A cord of three strands is not quickly broken. For years I took great pride in being a self-made man but eventually came to understand the power of a team. A team can have much greater impact than an individual. Determine the gifts of your teammates, get them on the right seats on the bus, and together you can make great things happen. The joy of seeing my other teammates grow and develop has provided me with some of my greatest satisfaction in life.

The last point to consider is that courage often results in great personal sacrifice. Look at what happened to the families of the 56 signers of the Declaration of Independence. Five were captured by the British as traitors and tortured before they died. Twelve had their homes ransacked and burned. Two lost their sons serving in the Revolutionary Army, another had two sons captured. Nine died from wounds or hardships of the Revolutionary War.

Carter Braxton of Virginia, a wealthy planter and trader, saw his ships swept from the seas by the British Navy. He sold his home and properties to pay his debts, and he died in rags.

Thomas McKean was so hounded by the British that he was forced to move his family almost constantly. He served in the Congress without pay, and his family was kept in hiding. His possessions were taken from him, and poverty was his reward. Vandals or soldiers looted the properties of Dillery, Hall, Clymer, Walton, Gwinnett, Heyward, Rutledge, and Middleton.

At the battle of Yorktown, Thomas Nelson, Jr., noted that the British General Cornwallis had taken over the Nelson home for his headquarters. He quietly urged General George Washington to open fire. The home was destroyed, and Nelson died bankrupt.

Francis Lewis had his home and properties destroyed. The enemy jailed his wife, and she died within a few months. John Hart was driven from his wife's bedside as she was dying. Their 13 children fled for their lives. His fields and his gristmill were laid to waste. For more than a year, he lived in forests and caves, returning home to find his wife dead and his children vanished. A few weeks later, he died from exhaustion and a broken heart. Norris and Livingston suffered similar fates. These were not wild-eyed, rabble-rousing ruffians. They were soft-spoken folks of means and education. They were people living for something greater than themselves. They were men and women of courage.

SUMMARY

"Success is not final and failure is seldom fatal; it is the courage to continue that counts." This statement, often attributed to Winston Churchill, must guide our efforts to truly serve people. If we are to serve people well, we must provide the vision to see what *should* be done, the *humility* to believe that with faith in God it *can* be done, and the courage to persevere until it *is* done.

True service is much more than a token gesture of charity typically motivated by our desire to assuage the guilt we feel for not truly serving our fellow man. Serving people demands that we steward our LIFE, our labor, our influence, our financial resources, and our expertise for creating a strong connection with the people we are striving to serve. And connecting will demand our time, our talent, and our treasure. It's messy, it's costly, its time consuming, it's emotionally draining, it's physically exhausting, but Jesus did it for us. Let's follow His example and willingly do it for others. Serving people in a deep, authentic way requires the steward leader to provide vision, humility, and courage to a team effort. The character trait required of a steward leader is CONNECTION. Let's update our high impact model now that we have taken an in-depth look at the second key principle, serving people.

END OF CHAPTER REFLECTION

Reflect and then elaborate on what you think God's vision for your LIFE is.

_____

_____

_____

_____

_____

_____

_____

_____

Would you describe your service to others as superficial or deep and authentic? What will you do to be a better servant?

_____

_____

_____

_____

_____

_____

_____

_____

_____

Notes

Work hard but pray harder. Daily prayer will calm you, motivate you, and sustain you.

Brice Butler

CHAPTER 5

THE HIGHEST STANDARD – PURSUING EXCELLENCE

"Excellence Honors God and inspires man."

WE STARTED BY FOCUSING ON PURPOSE, and now we are delving into passion. As we review the graphic, we see that our purpose in life is to honor God -- the center of our graphic. We honor God by pursuing the virtues of *truth, faith*, and *character*. In the previous chapter, we tackled the first of the three principles that make up our passion in LIFE; Serving People. The key to serving people was virtuous leadership, which we defined as providing *vision, humility* and *courage* to a team effort. The vision to see what *should* be done, the humility to believe that it *can* be done, and the courage to persevere until it *is* done. The primary character trait of a leader who serves is the ability to connect with those they lead.

Turning to the next principle, I want you to see how it is related to serving. Connection is a powerful tool for us as leaders, but connection without competence typically gives us a fast start and a poor finish. Connection gets us in the game, but competence keeps us in the game. Competence is the *expertise, innovation*, and *discipline* required to maximize the impact of our God-given talent and imbue it with excellence. Serving people requires leadership; pursuing excellence requires management. We lead people by serving. We manage processes with excellence. The uncompromising pursuit of excellence is essential for a high-impact life, because excellence honors God and inspires the people we serve. Excellence is the result of a virtuous manager bringing expertise, innovation, and discipline to a team effort.

UNDERSTANDING EXCELLENCE

Excellence can be defined as possessing good qualities in high degree, something that allows us to stand out and apart from the crowd. We must not confuse excellence with extravagance. I have seen this mistake made too many times, and it happens because we miss the fact that motivation is the difference between excellence and extravagance. If my motivation to excel is to bring attention to myself, to honor me, then it is arrogance, not excellence. And arrogance leads to extravagance. But if my motivation is to honor God, to excel for a reason greater than myself, then serving, producing, even consuming, can be done with excellence.

I have friends who own homes in beautiful places. If you didn't know them and their desire to honor God by serving people with such an asset, you would say they are extravagant. But when you see how they use it to restore the emotionally broken, give rest to the weary, and share the Good News, you see how they use this asset for excellence.

We must also understand that excellence is not defined by culture. When our purpose is to glorify ourselves instead of God, we are susceptible to allowing culture to dictate what is excellent. The phone we use, the car we drive, the neighborhood we live in, if not properly motivated, become extravagance and not excellence.

Nor is excellence defined by the cost of the object or service. Excellence is a state of mind. Excellence is doing the best you can, where you are, with what you have, for the glory of God. I spend a fair amount of time in developing countries, and I frequently see families living with profound excellence on three dollars per day. They don't have expensive assets, but they maintain and use whatever they *do* have with great excellence. I have seen excellent mud huts, and I have also seen broken down, dirty, trashy mud huts. The difference occurs because of the state of mind of the steward, not the dollar value of the asset.

> *Excellence is doing the best you can with the resources you have for the intent of glorifying God.*

The bottom line is that excellence is defined by God Himself. Psalm 8 tells us His name is excellent. In 2 Samuel, we learn that His work is excellent. Romans 12 tells us His will is excellent. Psalms 36 (KJV) proclaims that His loving-kindness is excellent. And Isaiah asserts that His salvation is excellent. In every way, God is excellent, and He defines what is excellent for us and in us.

THE IMPORTANCE OF EXCELLENCE

Excellence inspires us. Are you a Chick-fil-A fan? Most people I know are. The reason is because Chick-fil-A loves excellence. They serve a tasty chicken sandwich in a clean restaurant with unbelievable service. What an inspiration to hear a teenage server say, "My pleasure!" Chick-fil-A understands that pursuing excellence honors God and creates great customers.

My favorite place to buy gas is QuikTrip, a chain of 600 convenience stores located throughout the United States. The layout and cleanliness of their stores, the quality of their products, their constant innovation to serve me better, and the speed with which they check me out and count my money is astounding. I will drive miles out of the way to be served with excellence.

All of us love excellence. It's the driving ideal that makes capitalism work. When companies compete for your business by offering a better product at a fair price, we all win. Striving for excellence is good business.

Excellence inspires us – and I pursue it – because it honors God. *"But just as you excel in everything . . ."* (2 Corinthians 8:7). This includes our faith, our speech, our knowledge, and particularly, our generosity. Excellence should be part of everything we do.

ACHIEVING EXCELLENCE

If excellence is possessing great qualities in high degree and the reason to be excellent is to honor God and inspire others, how is excellence achieved? As we discussed in the last chapter, the driving force in serving people is connection. Connected leaders bring vision, humility, and courage to a team effort.

On the other hand, the essential driving force required to achieve excellence is competence. Competent managers bring *expertise, innovation,* and *discipline* to a coordinated effort. A culture of service is created when we lead people. A culture of excellence is created when we manage processes. Too many leaders fail because they think they should manage people when they should manage processes and *lead* people. If we are to create excellence in our lives and organizations, we must focus on these three critical virtues; *expertise, innovation,* and *discipline.* If implemented and managed well, these virtues will answer the three critical questions our followers want answered: What do you want me to do? How am I doing? Will you help me become better?

> *Too many leaders fail because they think they should manage people when they should manage processes and lead people.*

Too often we assume that the people we lead will somehow magically become who we desire them to be. The truth is that they cannot attain their highest level of excellence unless we lead with vision, humility, and courage, providing oversight and management of the work they perform through expertise, innovation, and discipline. As we pursue excellence, we must equip their minds with expertise, fill their hearts with an innovative spirit, and teach their hands to execute with great discipline. Let's look at each.

PURSUE
EXCELLENCE

EXPERTISE

Expertise is displaying a special skill or knowledge derived from study, training, or experience. Studies have shown that the most important way to achieve excellent performance in fields such as sports, music, professions, and scholarship is to practice. Achievement of excellence in such fields commonly requires years of dedication and tens of thousands of hours of effort. Expertise takes time!

Because of the significant time investment required to develop expertise, we should assess whether the investment is likely to pay off. We start with vision to ensure that the *what* and *why* are compelling before we develop the how. Otherwise, we could give years to developing expertise that we later realize is not aligned with God's calling on our life.

Expertise follows vision and is informed by wisdom. Wisdom is expertise that has been filtered through a moral grid. And for those of us who are Christians, that moral grid is God's word. Being an expert in distributing pornography is not wise, because it violates God's moral code. As you become an expert, also make sure you are becoming wise. Expertise often follows a God-given talent. Several chapters in Exodus reveal the Lord telling Moses how to build the tabernacle and all of its furnishings for worship. Then in Exodus 31:1-11 God tells Moses that He has chosen certain people to complete specific tasks. Speaking of one of them in verse 3, He says, "*I have filled him with the Spirit of God, with skill, ability and knowledge in all kinds of crafts.*"

We believe that just as God has created each of us with unique DNA, personality traits, and fingerprints, He has given each of us special skills and abilities. My parents spent thousands of dollars and endured a lot of heartache attempting to make a piano player out of me, but it simply wasn't my gifting.

Take the extra time and energy it requires for you to determine your God-given skills. And I cannot emphasize this enough: if you have teenage children, don't live vicariously through them by attempting to make them all the things you only dreamed of being. Find *their* passion, find *their* natural gifting and help them perfect it.

THE IMPORTANCE OF EXPERTISE

Character without competence results in failure. Expertise is essential if you are to have great impact. In Psalm 78:72, David speaks of expertise (competence) and character, "*So he shepherded them according to the integrity of his heart, and guided them with his skillful hands*" (NASB). Your competence gives you credibility, and your character sustains your credibility. You can't be credible unless you have developed expertise. You must know your business. People won't follow someone who does not know his or her job and how to do it.

Success requires expertise. Proverbs 22:29 says, "*Do you see a man skilled in his work? He will serve before kings*" (NIV, 1996). Ezekiel 28:5 says, "By your great skill in trading you have increased your wealth." But the end of the verse contains a warning for those who gain expertise and its rewards: "and because of your wealth your heart has grown proud." The acquisition of expertise will allow you to accomplish great things, but if those accomplishments are done for yourself, they will ultimately result in pride. Remember, a full head (expertise) without a faith-filled heart (character) leads to arrogance.

> *Expertise without character leads to arrogance.*

Finally, we should pursue and increase our expertise because it is a great example of stewardship. Colossians 3:23 says, "*Whatever you do, work at it with all your heart, as working for the Lord, not for human masters.*" Our goal in being an expert is always to honor God.

ACHIEVING EXPERTISE

Gaining expertise in any field begins with increased understanding and then engaging all three aspects of your being; your head, your heart, and your hands. Start by understanding who you are. Determine your sweet spot, your natural giftings. Assess how God has shaped you, and make sure you choose wisely how and on what you spend your time. Then pursue not only expertise, but wisdom. Make sure you are seeing things from God's perspective.

Second, search your heart to make sure your motivation for becoming an expert is God-honoring and not self-serving. Determine your motivation. Seek humility as you gain more expertise. And remember, expertise done for its own sake is not excellence, it is arrogance.

Third, make the commitment to pay the price. Perspective, preparation, and pain precede productivity. Be a problem solver; be teachable; worry about detail; be self-disciplined. Focus on the goal. Do not be led astray by distractions or other opportunities; say no to the good, so you can say yes to the best. Do not be distracted by people with impure motives, and don't be distracted because of fear. Always remember: if you know your purpose, the significance of your calling will overcome the fear of failure.

Last, pursue expertise with all your strength. If you are going to spend 10,000 hours to become an expert, it will take a significant commitment. Jesus spent thirty years in preparation for three years of service. Be prepared to face the obstacles that accompany any pursuit of expertise. Whether slothfulness, procrastination, arrogance, or other enemies of excellence, establish good habits and be prepared for the temptation to compromise that will inevitably come your way. Once you have equipped your mind with expertise, the next step toward excellence is to fill your heart with the spirit of innovation.

INNOVATION

Innovation means "to renew or change." Innovation results in better or more effective products, processes, technologies, or ideas. Innovation is creative adaptation in the pursuit of convenience, efficiency, and effectiveness. Innovation transforms expertise into goods and services that are a cut above the average. Innovation allows you to connect with your kids or in-laws in ways you never thought possible. It transforms products, relationships, companies, families, churches, and communities. Innovation is about taking risk, and by that I mean taking hold of a prayed-up, planned-up, and prepared-for opportunity. It is a powerful tool in the building of a high-impact LIFE.

Innovation is the enemy of the status quo. You, your company, your church, and your family are either growing or dying. If you think the status quo is fine, if you think we will just ride it out, you are not really living; you are dying. My son likes to say, "living things grow, and growing things change." Change is inevitable, so deal with it. The other option is to live a lackluster life fading into the sunset of mediocrity. Look around you. Innovation is everywhere, and it has made this chunk of rock we live on a pretty neat place to live. What would you do without your smart phone? What if our Founding Fathers hadn't dreamed about economic, social, and spiritual freedom? What if Bill Bright hadn't pursued the *Jesus* film? A recent study by Accenture revealed that more than 90 percent of executives believe that the long-term success of their organization's strategy depends on their ability to develop new ideas. Innovation allows you to have real impact. One of my favorite Bible stories is the healing of the paralytic in Mark 2. Here you have four guys caring for one of their friends who is paralyzed. They have heard about this fellow Jesus who can heal. They know if they can simply get their friend to him he will be healed. The problem is that everyone else in the village had the same idea and there was simply no way to get to Jesus through the crowds. Did they pack their bags and head home? No way. They huddled up and went to work on the problem. They began to innovate. They climbed on top of the house where Jesus was, dug a hole in the roof, and lowered their paralyzed friend right down in front of Jesus.

An amazing thing happened. When Jesus saw their innovation, what He defined as *their faith*, he said to the paralytic, "*Son, your sins are forgiven.*" Innovation is faith in action. It allows you to think out of the box. Innovation is also risky, requiring you to put faith to work in ways that will stretch it – and you.

Perhaps the most compelling reason you should innovate is because God is the ultimate innovator and we were designed in His image. He created us to innovate. Walk outside and spend thirty minutes with God. Marvel at His unlimited creativity and the fact that you were made in His image. You and I have untapped creative, innovative, abilities. We simply need to use them.

THE INNOVATIVE SPIRIT

The starting point of innovation is concluding that you need it. If you are tired of a dysfunctional family, or your company isn't growing, or your church is stagnant, or your personal life is a wreck, decide to change it. Whatever the reason, quit complaining and talking about the problem and start designing the solution with an innovative attitude. Essential in this process is not just acknowledging you need it but coming to the point where you are seeking it. Matthew 7:7-8 encourages us, "*Ask and it will be given to you; seek and you will find; knock and the door will be opened to you. For everyone who asks receives; the one who seeks finds; and to the one who knocks, the door will be opened.*" Ask God to give you insight. Seek the best solution by learning and studying what is working for others. And last, knock on the door; when it opens, take some risk and walk through it.

I am a natural risk taker. I like new ideas, new deals, new ways to do things better. Since it is easy for me to pull the trigger on a new innovative venture, I subject it to a three-step test. First I try to make sure I have faithfully asked God by spending lots of time in prayer. Second, I try to make sure that what I am seeking to do is based on sound, thoughtful preparation that has been done with the utmost diligence. And third, when I knock on the door, I try to remember just to knock. With patience. Not brute force.

More than once in my life I have thought that I should do this or do that. When it came time to knock and the door didn't open, I ramped up the knocking. The next thing I knew I was actually kicking in the door. And what I found on the other side was not what I had envisioned – certainly not what I wanted. I've learned the hard way to knock and wait till the door opens. If it doesn't open, I go back to my chair, pray more, plan more, prepare more, and innovate more. The reason the door doesn't open just might be that God is protecting us from implementing an innovative idea too soon. If the door doesn't open, perhaps we are not yet ready to proceed.

We need God to supply us with an innovative spirit, because innovation isn't easy. For some it comes more naturally, but for many it hardly comes at all. Here are some statistics on those who innovate. Three percent of the world are true innovators, thirteen percent are early adopters, sixty-eight percent are in the mushy middle, and thirteen percent of us never get it. The true innovators and the early adopters are the ones who totally believe in the innovation. They are the ones who stand in line for six hours to buy the first iPhone.

If you are not a true innovator, and most of us aren't, at least be on the hunt to see what others are doing and try to be an innovative early adopter. Study your competitors and understand the major trends and where they are going. If you can't solve the problem, if you don't have the ability to innovate, then find someone who can. While you may not be a creative genius, you can be the catalyst that evokes the skills of others into building an innovative culture. You must understand that collaboration is essential, failure is not fatal, and uncertainty will always be present. That said, you can devise a disciplined process that will manage the data, mitigate the risks, and drive you to the best solution in the shortest amount of time.

> *Collaboration is essential, failure is not fatal, and uncertainty will always be present.*
> Quote Adapted from Winston Churchill

One last thought when considering your need for innovation: make sure you have a very clear idea of what the problem is and understand what the final idea should look like. When Steve Jobs developed the iPod, his end idea was to have "1,000 songs in my pocket." A laser focus is critical to successful innovation.

We have come to understand that expertise and innovation are critical in our pursuit of excellence. Once we have equipped our minds with expertise and had our hearts filled with the spirit of innovation, we must set our hands to the task of exercising discipline. For an inspiring example of personal discipline in the pursuit of excellence, we turn to Brice Butler, NFL wide receiver for the Arizona Cardinals.

> *A mentor once told me that good is the enemy of great. Every year many professional athletes reach the end of their career. Their fans and teammates remember most of them as merely good players. Then there are the few who achieve a level of greatness within their sport, especially the NFL. Why? What makes the difference? The road to become a great player is one far less traveled. Great players differentiate themselves from good players in very distinct ways: their habits. Great players log countless hours – in fact, countless*

years – dedicating themselves to developing and perfecting these habits. They show up early and leave late. Great players find satisfaction in the extra reps. Great players make sacrifice a habit. They constantly force themselves to trade good habits for great habits.

If you think about it, most aspects of our lives are comprised of habits. Our relationships and jobs have many habits woven into the day-to-day. In my current job of football, I constantly submit myself to habits I believe will take my game to the next level, because football is not only my job but also what I am passionate about. Honestly, I can't remember a time when I was not passionate about football and pursuing high-impact habits.

I am extremely blessed and thankful for the opportunity to play and compete at a high level. I realize that how long I play at this high level is primarily determined by what I do off the field. Along my journey to the NFL, I have intentionally neglected many opportunities off the field to set myself up to pursue the greatest ones on the field.

I take a unique mindset to my day-to-day diet, exercise, and rest. When I set a training goal to improve myself as an athlete, I have a direct focus on what and how I want to achieve that training goal. For example, if I set a goal to improve my strength and speed, yet I am constantly eating junk food, staying up and going out late with buddies, then I will make little to no progress. However, if I view these distractions as enemies to achieving my goals, I will intentionally neglect them, putting me on the path to achieve my goal. I replace junk food with a nutritional meal, go to bed on time, and spend time with my friends when it doesn't rob my rest.

Learning to delay instant gratification is half the battle. The *athletes who have achieved greatness have left a wake of intentional neglect and sacrifice of lesser values behind them. Without this mindset you will constantly be thrown off course with your goals.*

Identifying aspects of your life that are potential enemies to your goals helps you prioritize where you need to develop and spend your time. This also makes you very aware of your weaknesses.

This mindset has not come to me naturally. Instead, it is one I have had to learn – sometimes the hard way. In college, I started to see some of my natural ability fade because of the distractions I was giving myself to. You see, I grew up in Atlanta in a blessed home. My parents are still married, and they love and serve the Lord, structuring their parenting accordingly. My dad played in the NFL in the 80s and then became an ordained minister. My mom still serves as a spiritual advisor to Charles Stanley and his organization. They provided me with incredible biblical instruction and teaching. My parents modeled intentional neglect to show us how to grow in our relationship with the Lord.

"Train up a child in the way he should go; even when he is old he will not depart from it" (Proverbs 22:6). That is the philosophy my parents used in raising my siblings and me. We grew up with a lot of discipline. We couldn't do everything we wanted to do. My parents urged us to stay the course and adhere to a strict moral standard. As kids, I remember thinking, This sucks. I don't get to do anything fun. I remember when I went to USC to play wide receiver: Finally, I am completely free to make my own decisions!

Those decisions were not always the greatest. Although I had been a Christian since a young age, when I got to college I really struggled just doing my own thing. Once your purpose starts slipping, you start doing things that sabotage what you are passionate about.

During my first two years in college, I thought what I was doing was just having a good time and having fun. But I drifted from great and settled for good. Slowly, I drifted from being around others who had a close relationship with the Lord, and before long I was no longer attending a solid church. I got to a point where I realized this was not me or how I had been raised. I couldn't look at myself in the mirror.

Those first two years were dark. Just going along with the crowd and doing everything they were doing off the field impacted my focus on the field. I wasn't performing as well as I wanted to during practices or games. All aspects of my life were affected. Eventually, I felt empty and realized that this was not how I wanted to live my life.

I was tired of doing what I was doing, and I knew I shouldn't be doing it. This built to the point that I was hungry for fellowship with other believers. I remembered the high school visit I had made to USC with my parents. We had visited a good church that I continued to attend for a while, but not for a long time now. I decided to give it a try again.

The memories flooded my mind as soon as I walked through the door – how solid the people were, how life giving it was – to me personally. The pastor was a younger man, someone I could easily relate to. He really helped my walk with the Lord. I saw that there were other people my age who were living for Christ, and it inspired me to do it again. I planted myself in the church. Met everybody. This was huge for me down the road, because they later helped me find a church family when I played for the Cowboys.

Our spirit and flesh are always at war with each other, and eventually I realized that I wanted to live a life of impact, a life of greatness. This church family helped me root myself in God's word, an essential part of great impact.

Greatness is not performing at a high level just to make yourself great. It is to make the King of kings great. I've been blessed with this platform to be a blessing to others. That is true greatness. As a kid I was taught that "to whom much is given, much is required" (Luke 12:48). This is why I facilitate youth football camps, invest in my community, read to kids at school — to inspire them to achieve great things. This platform has allowed me to make an impact for Christ with those who might not have a very receptive ear. That is greatness.

My purpose is to do the works Jesus talked about in John 14:12 — even greater works than He did — which for me is leading people to Him. That's what we are here to do as believers. Whatever platform I have, I am going to try to lead others to Jesus. That is why I am here. You are not here just to get saved and sit in your house. You are here to be the man or woman who helps others understand who Christ is.

This is my purpose, and football is what I do, but football is not what defines me as a person. Christ defines me as a person.

HIGH IMPACT HABIT
Work hard but pray harder. Daily prayer will calm you, motivate you, and sustain you.

Brice's story is an interesting combination of disciplines. He began by describing the necessary self-discipline needed to achieve excellence. But when his focus shifted to the distractions around him and he lost that self-discipline, God had to step in and provide the necessary loving discipline to draw him back.

DISCIPLINE

To many of us, discipline is an ugly ten-letter word! Not many of us cherish it in either of its two meanings. The noun form of the word means the practice of following a code of conduct or regimen of activity. "Discipline will make you a healthy person." The verb form means to punish or penalize for the sake of enforcing obedience and perfection of moral character, to impose order. "You need to discipline your son before he becomes a truant." Unfortunately for those of us who don't impose the noun form of discipline in our lives, the verb form will usually follow. If my father told me once, he told me a dozen times, "A disciplined life is a happy life." I know it's true, but that doesn't make it easy.

DISCIPLINE AND SUCCESS

Discipline leads to success because it is the key to becoming a person of Character, Competence, Commitment, and Connection. And if you are a person who possesses those four attributes, you will be a person who leads a high-impact LIFE. Here is what God's word says about the benefits to living a disciplined life.

1. Discipline is a sign of God's love. Proverbs 3:11-12, "*My son, do not despise the Lord's discipline . . . because the Lord disciplines those he loves.*"

2. Discipline is a smart thing to embrace. Proverbs 12:1, "*Whoever loves discipline loves knowledge, but whoever hates correction is stupid.*"

3. Discipline leads to profit. Proverbs 14:23, "*All hard work brings a profit, but mere talk leads only to poverty.*"

4. The lack of discipline is deadly. Proverbs 5:23, "*For lack of discipline they will die, led astray by their own great folly.*"

5. Discipline is the way to life. Proverbs 10:17, "*Whoever heeds discipline shows the way to life, but whoever ignores correction leads others astray.*"

6. Discipline is a blessing from God. Psalm 94:12, "*Blessed is the one you discipline, Lord, the one you teach from your law.*"

7. Discipline is required from parents. Proverbs 23:13, "*Do not withhold discipline from a child.*"

8. Discipline is part of acquiring the truth. Proverbs 23:23, "*Buy the truth and do not sell it; get wisdom, discipline and understanding*" (NIV, 1996).

PRACTICING A DISCIPLINED LIFE

Self-discipline starts with the conviction that you must make a change in your life; you get to the point where you say, "I have to change the way I'm living." On any given day we employ 160 inmates in a maximum-security prison. These men are living in a desert bereft of human flourishing. They have no economic, social, or spiritual wellbeing. This often leads to a severely broken person with absolutely no vision or hope for life. Time after time we have seen that the ones who succeed in this harsh environment come to the point of great conviction to change their lives and have the discipline to follow through.

Conviction must be followed by a deep and meaningful commitment to be disciplined. This usually happens only with the help of the Holy Spirit providing us with the courage and stamina to make the change. 2 Tim 1:7 says, *"For God did not give us a spirit of timidity, but a spirit of power, of love and of self-discipline"* (NIV, 1996).

A key tool in helping you move from an undisciplined life to one of discipline is an annual personal plan. For the last forty years, I have completed an annual plan, and I will tell you it has revolutionized my life. It allows me to understand the difference between the urgent and the important. It helps me prioritize my life and lets me maximize the most precious of all things: time. It provides a tool for me to think long term, even to the point of thinking about today in terms of eternity. I have found it to be an essential tool in the pursuit of discipline. Section four of this book, Launch The Plan, will lead you through the journey of developing your own personal plan.

A second important tool required for a disciplined life is accountability. Whether with my older mentors, my close friends, or the advisors who help me navigate the uncharted waters of a new entrepreneurial venture, their help in holding me accountable is essential for me to maintain discipline. Proverbs 27:17 says, *"As iron sharpens iron, so one person sharpens another."*

A third indispensable tool is the discipline of establishing a rhythm of life. Essential to this rhythm is the development of certain personal disciplines that are key to high-impact living. The highest priority is to establish the spiritual discipline of a morning and evening time with God. In doing so, God will help you to focus on the important instead of the urgent.

Your first and last activity of the day should be to spend time *being* with Him. It is a listening time, not a *doing* time. Use this time for prayer, listening, and personal meditation. By being disciplined about my morning and evening time with God, I can block out the distractions of life before I go to bed, allowing my head and heart to meditate on His thoughts. This daily time in God's word, prayer, and Scripture memory is the essential ingredient in a high-impact LIFE because it allows us to commune with and hear from God Himself.

We must also establish the disciplines of great relationships. Relational disciplines help me to love my wife and spend time with my family and friends. Great relationships also allow others to speak truth into my life. I have a small contingent of very close friends who do this; they know me so well that they can sense when my life balance is out of kilter. And with a simple probing question or a bit of truth spoken in love, they cut right to the heart of the problem and make me aware of my need.

Many other important disciplines come to mind. Stewarding the assets God has given me to manage requires the economic disciplines of an annual budget and the monitoring of a personal balance sheet. Physical disciplines are required for us to take care of our body, our temple. Mental and emotional disciplines allow us to truly become experts in our vocations. Then there is the discipline of saying no. Of all the disciplines I try to exercise, this is the most difficult and always creates the most consternation in my life. It is so difficult to exercise in the moment but so blessed in the end.

SUMMARY

Excellence is powerful because it honors God and inspires men. Unfortunately, it seems as though it is becoming a lost art in today's culture. Our pursuit of pride, pleasure, and possessions often keeps us from experiencing true excellence. These distractions consume our time, talent, and resources, not allowing us to become the excellent people God created us to be. Aristotle said, "We are what we repeatedly do. Excellence, then, is not an act but a habit." Are you pursuing excellence in everything you do and seeking to honor God as a result? This must be our goal if we are to live the high-impact LIFE.

END OF CHAPTER REFLECTION

What does accountability look like for me?

_____

_____

_____

_____

_____

_____

_____

What does my day look like? How can I improve my routine?

_____

_____

_____

_____

_____

_____

_____

Identify an area where you are struggling and find mentors who are doing that thing well. Then do as they do.

Howard Dayton

CHAPTER 6

THE ULTIMATE CAREER – STEWARDING CAPITAL

"We make a living by what we get; we make a life by what we give."
Unknown

I PRAY THAT OVER THESE FIRST FIVE chapters you have been on a journey of personal transformation. It all begins when we discover what it means to love our purpose, which is to honor God. From there we focus on the principles of serving people and pursuing excellence. Honoring God is how we develop the *principles* that guide our life. Serving defines how we deal with the *people* in our life. Excellence is how we deal with the *processes* in our life.

As God works in us to shape our life and leadership according to these principles, we turn to the third and final principle to complete the high impact model: stewarding capital. This is how we perceive and care for the many tangible and intangible property and profits God has given us to steward. The acrostic LIFE will help you remember the major personal asset categories: our Labor (time), our Influence (tribe), our Financial capital (treasure), and our Expertise (talent).

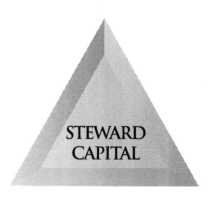

STEWARD
CAPITAL

DEFINING STEWARDSHIP

Stewardship is the careful management of something entrusted to our care. It demands that we give thoughtful attention to the owner's intents and wishes for their property and capital.

Several Bible references, including 1 Chronicles 29, tell us that everything in the heavens and earth belongs to the Lord. We respond by taking care in how we spend our time, love the tribe we have been given to influence, manage our treasure, and pursue our talent. This includes everything from the last breath you just took, the family and friends you've been given, the material possessions you hold in trust, and even your relationship with God Himself. As I explained in Chapter 1, the transition from thinking like an owner to thinking like a steward was revolutionary for me: once I understood this concept, I made the commitment to stop living for me and start living for something greater than myself.

Stewardship also means refusing to hold on to the things that I previously associated with success. Instead, it is taking all of my life – my labor, influence, financial capital, and expertise – and laying them at the feet of Jesus, saying, "I'm all in." It's not about pursuing my success; it's not even about satisfied significance; it's about total surrender. I love that ageless hymn by Frances Havergal that so perfectly defines stewardship:

Take my life and let it be

Consecrated, Lord, to Thee.

Take my moments and my days,

Let them flow in endless praise.

Take my hands and let them move

At the impulse of Thy love.

Take my feet and let them be

Swift and beautiful for Thee.

Take my voice and let me sing,

Always, only for my King.

Take my lips and let them be

Filled with messages from Thee.

Take my silver and my gold,

Not a mite would I withhold.

Take my intellect and use

Every pow'r as Thou shalt choose.

Take my will and make it Thine,

It shall be no longer mine.

Take my heart, it is Thine own,

It shall be Thy royal throne.

Take my love, my Lord, I pour

At Thy feet its treasure store.

Take myself and I will be

Ever, only, all for Thee.

Living as a faithful steward means taking all we are, all we have, and all we can be, surrendering all of it at the feet of Jesus. If you are focused on who you are, how you live, and what you own, you are thinking like an owner. If you are focused on the why, on living for something greater than yourself, you are thinking like a steward. Stewardship is moving from the pursuit of success to the freedom of surrender.

THE FREEDOM OF THE STEWARD

The world values and teaches that the purpose of life is to get all we can. Why should we think and live any differently? Well, to put it simply, because as a true follower of Jesus, we don't have a choice. Living as a steward is an outward demonstration of our inward faith. It's how we show the world that Christ has transformed our hearts and impacted our lives. The end game of stewarding capital is a LIFE of radical generosity, and our generosity literally defines who we are and whom we serve. It's the ultimate way we love our neighbors as ourselves.

God's command for us to be stewards, as with all of His commands, comes with a reward: living the LIFE of a faithful steward will set us free. We will know the truth, and the truth will set us free: free from the bondage of never having enough time, the bondage of poor relationships, the bondage of always desiring to have more stuff. It will set us free from the incessant drive to be accepted by the world. It frees us to take what we have and leverage it for eternal purposes. It frees us to take risks, to lead, and to enjoy the life God has given us.

Living a life of stewardship results in earthly contentment and eternal rewards. Can you imagine standing before the Creator of the universe at the end of your life and having Him personally commend you with the words, "Well done, good and faithful servant"? That is the destiny of the faithful steward.

THE LIFE OF THE STEWARD

One of the greatest misconceptions Christians hold is that stewardship is only for those with significant financial wealth because they are the only ones with assets to steward. To understand why this is such a distortion, let's go back to our LIFE acrostic. We all have a LIFE; Labor, Influence, Financial capital, and Expertise that can be stewarded.

As I look back on my life, I can honestly say that the people who have had the greatest impact on me were the people who did not have great financial wealth. Instead, these people poured their Labor (time), their Influence (relationships), and their Expertise (talent/wisdom) into me. And their impact on me has been monumental. As I mentioned earlier, I have had two mentors who have walked beside me for the last 40 years. Their wisdom, their insight, and their ability to speak truth into my life have demonstrated their unconditional love for me and impacted my life beyond measure. This has taught me that the stewardship of my time and talent will likely have more impact than the stewardship of my treasure.

LEADERSHIP VERSUS MANAGEMENT

The age old $64 million question is this: "Are you a leader or a manager?" I would take you back to the last two sections you just finished reading and highlight two very important statements.

- A connected leader leads people.

- A competent manager manages processes.

Let me now add a third.

- A virtuous steward stewards the enterprise.

A virtuous steward artfully brings these two disciplines of leading and managing into a finely tuned balance that fosters great relational capital through vision, humility, and courage – at the same time creating impeccable operating excellence through expertise, innovation, and discipline. The result is a high-impact enterprise.

All of us have been gifted uniquely. Some have a natural bent toward leading; others have a bent toward managing. Determine who you are and maximize the gift you have been given. Additionally, find another person who is gifted in the areas you are not. It is important to understand that the further up the responsibility ladder you climb, the more balanced you will have to become in both leadership and management techniques.

LEADERSHIP VS MANAGEMENT ILLUSTRATED

*So he **fed** them (connection) according to the **integrity** (character) of his heart, And **guided** them (commitment) with the **skillfulness** (competence) of his hands.*

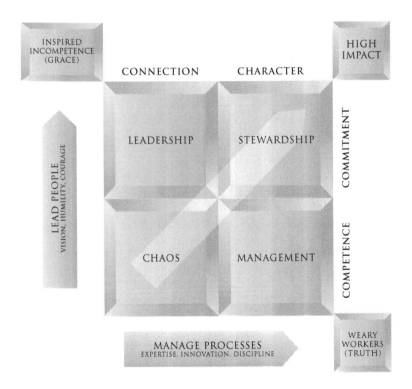

CREATING CAPITAL

Let's look at how you create capital to steward, starting with the first triangle in our diagram, the Honor God triangle. The creation of capital that God will entrust to you to steward starts with the pursuit of truth – all truth, not just spiritual truth. It is the truth of the marketplace, physical truth, emotional truth, and of course, spiritual truth. As you begin to fill your head with truth, you will begin to believe with your heart what you are learning with your head. You start to become a person of faith.

As you believe, you begin to take faith-filled action, which is character. As you exercise character, God reveals to you His vision for what you could accomplish. You have now transitioned to the second triangle of Serving People. As this vision becomes more defined, you begin to exercise humility, understanding that your role in it is not your own creation but a gift from God Himself. He also provides great courage in response to your knowing the truth, believing in faith, and acting with character. This courage results in action that drives you to the pursuit of excellence, the third triangle.

As you pursue excellence, you will become an expert or a person of great knowledge in your field. As expertise is created and grows, it typically demands greater innovation, which allows for greater excellence and a greater impact in the marketplace. Expertise and innovation driven by the discipline to become ever better will result in the creation of a LIFE, (Labor, Influence, Financial capital, Expertise) that can be stewarded to have even greater impact for God's kingdom. Once God has entrusted you with one or more forms of capital, it is essential that you become a great steward of them, using them to honor God in all you do.

Let me give you a practical example of how this works. I grew up on a farm in central Kansas, and yet I always had a desire to be an entrepreneur. At the age of 29 I became restless in a predictable banking job, and I began to pursue other available careers. As I began to pursue the various options in the market place, I learned more about what I could do technically and what I wanted to do emotionally. I began to understand the truth of the marketplace, and it drove me to have faith that my idea might work.

I then stepped out in faith – exercising character – by taking various actions that led to a confirmation of my business idea. Once I had the idea, I began developing a vision for what I might be able to accomplish. The more I pursued the vision, the more hope and humility began to well up in me.

Now I needed to exercise the courage to start the business. As I persevered, I became more knowledgeable about my business. I became an expert. More expertise resulted in more success, which created the need for more innovation, which led to more business, which then required more discipline.

As I became more disciplined and better at what I did, I was given more capital to steward. Today, after 35 years of this journey, we have been given not only financial assets to steward, but more importantly, expertise and influence so that we can have even greater impact on the business community.

Now that we understand our call to be faithful stewards, let's look at what it means to pursue the three virtues that will equip us to become great stewards: Perspective, Integrity, and Generosity.

PERSPECTIVE

The word "perspective" is derived from the Latin word *perspectivum*, meaning to see clearly, to look through and see the interrelationship between the subject and its parts. Put another way, it is the capacity to view things in their true relative importance to everything else. To be a steward is to understand the relationship between you and your Creator. It is to grasp the fact that He is the omnipotent God, the Creator and Owner of everything.

With that understanding, we acknowledge that we are created in His image for the purpose of glorifying Him and enjoying Him forever. When we come to this life-changing perspective, we are on our way to becoming the stewards God created us to be. God has given to His people the magnificent task of managing, tending, caring for, and stewarding this great creation of His.

I recall an incident that taught me about perspective. I had just graduated from college with a degree in business and had taken a job with a local bank. On my second day on the job, the owner of the bank came to me and asked if I would fly to Canada and represent a business transaction worth many millions of dollars. I was elated.

I remember sitting in the first-class cabin all decked out in my brand new suit and starched white shirt enjoying a filet mignon and dazzling sunset as we flew along the great Rocky Mountains. I couldn't believe my good fortune – *what an incredible job I have!*

A limousine awaited my arrival. I had lunch the next day at the exclusive Calgary Club before being whisked off to the bank where again I was given the royal treatment. Little did they know I was just a management trainee acting as the pickup man to escort a $14 million check back to the US.

Flying home the following day, I had the unexpected experience of looking down and seeing my father's farm, the very place I had spent my entire childhood. Even at this high altitude I knew it was his farm because it sat next to the Cheyenne Bottoms, a large body of water located in the middle of Kansas. To my amazement, I could see my dad's tractor with a big cloud of dust trailing it. Picture it: 35,000 feet below is my father plowing a field in a cloud of 95-degree dust, and here I am in air-conditioned first-class comfort with a $14 million check in my pocket, eating filet mignon, and wheeling and dealing in the world of high finance. And it was only my second day on the job! I thought to myself, *I have made it.*

Isn't it interesting how a few externals can change our perspective? My inflated ego at that moment made me feel like a big shot. But my dad, a speck on the tractor below, was one with the right perspective. Little did I realize how my life and my perspective would change over the next twenty years.

What is your perspective on your life and work? Are you living your life as an owner or a steward? Remember, ownership is important to us, but stewardship is important to God. The depth of our character is reflected in the unequivocal conviction that God owns it all.

Consequently, we need to know God and His perspective so we can manage His creation as He sees fit. We need to understand His desires in order to serve Him faithfully and receive His authority to be stewards. As it says in Psalms 8:6, "*You made them [man] rulers over the works of your hands; you put everything under their feet.*"

Once we have taken on the mantle of stewardship, we are then required to be faithful. Paul tells us in 1 Corinthians 4:2, "*Now it is required that those who have been given a trust must prove faithful.*" The way we steward our life is a direct reflection of the truth, faith, and character we exercise as we strive to honor God. This perspective is so vitally important because it determines how we live. If you believe you are the owner, you will live by a different set of rules than if you are the steward.

Earlier in this book we discussed in length the importance of the why question. In this last principle of stewarding capital, I believe the why question is even more important. Stewardship becomes so poignant and so powerful because this is where the world will see you as being truly different. This is where you demonstrate that you are honoring God by serving people, pursuing excellence, and being a great steward. This is faith in action. This is where you can bear witness to a suspicious, unbelieving world that God-fearing, people-serving, excellence-pursuing followers of Jesus are the real deal. This is where you can lay down your life for others. This is where you can emotionally, physically, and spiritually demonstrate that you love your neighbor as yourself. This is stewardship.

Understanding the perspective of God's ownership is the only way to attain true contentment in life. Contentment is learned. It is a choice of the will. Paul says in Philippians 4:12, "*I know what it is to be in need, and I know what it is to have plenty. I have learned the secret of being content in any and every situation.*" Learning it and then exercising it result in a more intimate relationship with God the Father.

If perspective is having a clear mental understanding that God is the owner and we are His managers, what do we do with this bit of life-changing truth? We must believe it in our heart. We must exercise integrity with this unbelievable gift of stewardship that God has entrusted to us.

INTEGRITY

Integrity is the deep belief in and adherence to a moral code or set of ethical principles. Perspective is a head thing; integrity is a heart thing. Although it is easy for us to intellectually understand that God, as the creator of everything, is the owner of everything, it is a very different thing for us to allow that belief to drive the actions of our life. If we truly believed that "he who sows generously will reap generously," wouldn't we be out every day looking to spread generosity to everyone we encounter? If we truly believed that "*the borrower is servant to the lender*," wouldn't we avoid debt at almost every turn? If we truly believed that "*if we have food and clothing, we will be content*," wouldn't we cease the pursuit of so many frivolous activities that consume our time, talent, and energy?

One of the greatest hindrances to living a high-impact LIFE is that we don't believe what we know to be true. We don't exercise integrity. It takes great integrity and a strong faith to live out these truths that seem so countercultural. Give and it will be given back? Love your neighbor as yourself? These are not normal for humankind, and it takes a great deal of integrity – a radical, strong belief – to live them out. When it comes to money, I always prided myself on being a 90/10 guy. I wanted to make a lot of money so that my ten percent to God was a big number. And you can imagine what I was contemplating for the other ninety percent. But when I came to understand that it was really zero percent mine and one-hundred percent God's, it rocked my world. This move from success to surrender was monumental. Business deals that went south did not consume me for months on end, and those that were successful were viewed as works of God and not merely personal achievements. Peace of mind and contentment prevailed. The contentment, peace of mind, and pure enjoyment from being a generous person were things I had always longed for but had never been able to grasp.

One of my heroes is a man who has helped me understand God's perspective on money. Howard Dayton, founder of Compass – *finances God's way*, has provided us with this inspiring story of how God transformed his life to take what had been a weakness – his slavery to money – and make it a platform for reaching millions with the gospel and the message of financial freedom.

> *The dinner conversation around my childhood home often had to do with business or money. By the time I graduated from Cornell, I had one objective in life: to become as rich as I could, as quickly I could. I didn't care about people. I was dishonest in my business dealings. I just wanted to get rich. I moved straight to Orlando when Disney was first announced, because I thought it would be a great place to make a boat load of money.*

One of my first projects, the Caboose Restaurant, was a huge success. However, I realized that as much as I loved to create and pioneer new projects, I hated to manage them. During that experience I started to meet with a small group of successful business guys to find out how to be more effective and make more money. I knew they were very savvy business people, but there was also something else about them that was very attractive to me.

I didn't realize it at the time, but they were passionate about influencing lost guys, like me, for Christ. Thankfully, six months after I started to meet with them, I was introduced to Christ. My wife, Bev, met the Lord five weeks after I did.

The Lord allowed us to get plugged into a really amazing church that didn't pass the plate for offerings. I loved this, because at the time I didn't want to give any of my money away.

A short time later I became partners with a guy named Jim Seneff, a very mature believer. Jim came to me after a Christmas holiday and said, "I've been reading through Proverbs, and it says a lot about money. We don't know a lot of what the Bible says about money, so let's take as long as we need to and read through it to identify all the verses on the subject. I think we will be better off for the experience."

It took us a year to identify the 2,350 Bible verses dealing with money. This was back in 1973, before personal computers. Our method was to take paper and scissors, placing each verse onto the appropriate pile based on the themes we found. We had piles for God's ownership, generosity, debt, all kinds of topics. After a year of creating all these piles around the office, it took us another year to really dig into each verse and fine-tune the topics and corresponding verses. Finally, we finished organizing all 2,350 verses by category.

I've often thought about the command in Deuteronomy 17 instructing the king to write the law by hand, carry it with him, and read it daily. That is really what happened to me. I dug into the truth and what God had to say about money. And I was a different person coming out of that experience.

My life totally changed. Before, I hadn't realized that God owns everything. He is the one who gives us our skills, abilities and opportunities. We have responsibilities, and God has responsibilities. We often say that He has a part and we have a part. God's part is to be the owner and ultimate provider. Our part is to be faithful to handle His capital – entrusted to us – His way.

One example of God doing His part as provider: When the oil embargo halted the economy, our real estate business halted as well. Deals just weren't moving. But God provided one deal that took us only two weeks to work out. We bought ten acres for $2,000 an acre near Tampa. Six months and a day later, we sold that piece for $10,000 per acre.

I learned that as long as you are doing what God wants you to do, He is going to provide. So we worked two weeks and made enough to take care of us that year.

I became passionate about teaching others about a biblical approach to finances and God's capital. My partner and I would go once a month to conduct seminars for groups of pastors at various churches. God continued to press into my heart that He may be calling me to do this full time.

I approached my wife with the idea, and she was very encouraging, adding another twist to it. "Howard, what would you think of putting into practice at a very personal and practical level what you're preaching? What if we were to become financially free in our own lives? As long as we live modestly, we could get to the place where we won't need a salary or book royalties."

I thought this sounded great, and so we started the journey. It took us nine years to get financially free, to be completely out of debt and have the house paid for. My wife was driving a 17-year-old car – part of our lifestyle decisions – but we never regretted it for one second. We had a clear objective of becoming financially free so we could respond to God if He called us in any direction.

God continued to energize our commitment by impressing Esther 4:14 on us. "Who knows whether you have not come to the kingdom for such a time as this?" This led to me taking a step in faith to start Crown Ministries, which ultimately became Compass – finances God's way.

Knowing your calling with certainty is super important. I have been in three major situations where I've needed to know God's direction. On average, it took about six months to know for certain I was called. Each time it finally got to the point where I said, "Lord, I don't care what you want me to do, just show me."

Our part is to seek counsel, to be in the word, and to be surrendered. God's responsibility is to give us clarity in His perfect timing.

While I was still in business, my view was that I was totally in ministry. Yes, to have a profitable business takes a lot of effort. But I was really there to influence our staff, vendors, customers, and even our competition. When I made the transition to full-time ministry, it seemed like the only change was that I now had more time to devote to ministry. I had been in ministry all along.

A very influential book in my business/ministry life was Master Plan of Evangelism. This gave the blueprint for how Jesus did ministry. Jesus took ordinary guys and discipled them to such a level that they reproduced it, still affecting us some two thousand years later. So as I launched my platform, I focused on small groups, partnering with the local church to deliver a curriculum we designed to be easily transferable.

After launching the course, we saw that giving had increased by 69 percent, and debt had been significantly reduced. This, of course, was very encouraging. We also developed a clear vision for our community and encouraged others to do the same for their communities. Our goal was to have 10,000 people go through the study over a five-year period and experience an average debt reduction of 10,000 dollars en route to debt freedom.

We wanted to focus on a few leaders and multiply. The growth of our platform, however, wasn't an uninterrupted bell curve. It looked more like a stair step. We started to realize that the plateau times were opportunities to develop our internal leadership, materials, and processes. This was key to our growth.

What really catapulted our growth was when we merged with Larry Burkett, who had two million radio listeners weekly. This positioned us to land our product in 88 countries. Within just shy of a decade we expanded our reach to 50 million globally. None of this would have occurred without such a strong leadership team and unified global vision. We organized to find key people around the globe to focus on their country or beyond, to their continent. From 2002 to 2007, we went from just a few countries in Latin America to every place.

HIGH IMPACT HABIT

Identify an area where you are struggling and find mentors who are doing that thing well. Then do as they do.

When we understand with our mind that God owns it all — the right

perspective – and live it out with our heart – godly integrity –
then we will live a generous LIFE.

GENEROSITY

Generosity is the culmination of a high-impact LIFE. It is the
result of living for something greater than yourself. Generosity is the
virtue of giving good things to others freely and abundantly. It is the
willful, cheerful, stewardship of your LIFE; your time (Labor), tribe
(Influence through relationships), treasure (Financial capital), and
talent (Expertise). It is the antithesis of greed and the only antidote
for a self-serving life. If your purpose in life is to live for yourself,
the fruit will be greed. If your purpose in life is to live for something
greater than yourself, you will live a life of generosity.

Generosity is not a random idea or haphazard sporadic behavior;
rather, it is a basic, personal, moral, foundational orientation to life.
It not only represents good things given but also bad things rejected.
It's using your life to help rid the world of greed, racism, sexism,
and other malignant behaviors that harm us either personally or
corporately. Generosity involves not just giving abundantly to others
but giving those things that are good for others. Generosity always

intends to enhance the true well-being of those to whom it gives. It is the pursuit of what is good, true, and beautiful. Generosity is foundational and essential for humanity to flourish. Generosity also includes giving that goes far beyond the scope of financial assets: real difference makers such as time, attention, aid, encouragement, emotional availability, and more. True generosity is done with the sole motivation to bless another regardless of any benefits that may accrue to the giver.

> *True generosity is done with the sole motivation to bless another regardless of any benefits that may accrue to the giver.*

THE JOY OF GENEROSITY

Why would one be generous? Why would anyone want to give and steward their labor, influence, financial capital, and expertise at the risk of depleting their tangible and intangible assets for the sake of no gain? Here's why. Generosity is the gospel. A generous life allows us to be like Jesus. And what did Jesus do for us? He gave the ultimate sacrifice, His life.

Generosity is the result of gaining wisdom and maturity. As leaders, it allows us to rise above the petty skirmishes of life that highlight our own greed and pride. It is the one virtue that allows us to step out of the mushy middle of mediocrity and live a high-impact LIFE. Generosity is also contagious. My wife and I attended a Generous Giving Celebration several years ago. We were inspired to increase the spontaneity of our giving based on a personal story shared by one of the speakers. Soon after the conference, we encountered an opportunity to be spontaneously generous. That gift inspired others, which then inspired others, and the downline results have been nothing short of amazing. The exponential nature of generosity cannot be measured.

One thing I have learned is that generosity is also fun. Every so often we will give our employees cash to simply give away at their discretion for the purpose of getting them to experience the joy of generosity. The only requirement is that they email us with the story and any outcome. The stories we have heard about how the lives of both givers and receivers were changed brought great joy to us.

Last but certainly not least, generosity will set you free. It frees you from all the complexities of ownership. What you give requires no maintenance. There is no worry. You regain time. You develop new friends. And this freedom leads to great contentment: no regret for the past, no resentment in the present, no anxiety about the future. Generosity is freedom.

The challenge is that generosity is not a natural behavior for most of us. It is foreign and misaligned with our self-serving mentality. So how do we move from selfish owners to generous stewards? How do we move into this last monumental step of personal transformation? As with most major accomplishments in life, the strategy is usually straightforward, but the execution is excruciating.

As we delve into this all-important topic, I would challenge you to think of generosity not as a giving thing but as a living thing. Generosity will have the most impact if it is not just a part of our life but it is literally how we live LIFE. This is how Jesus lived. Living was giving. If we treat it as a bifurcated duty, as one of the many spiritual disciplines we need to check off our good Christian to-do list, it will lack the power and authenticity that is needed for it to have full impact. Generosity is not simply doing, it is being.

Remember that personal transformation starts with the conviction that a change, sometimes a dramatic change, is needed. It begins when we realize that we are not living LIFE to its fullest. This honest self-assessment leads to the deep conviction that we should move from being owners to stewards. Our journey of conversion to stewardship leads us to a commitment to live generously. We must understand this process of moving from conviction to conversion to commitment.

Let's start with conviction. Think about a time when you experienced the sensation of being prompted to do something for someone. It may have been a minor thing like helping an elderly person cross the street or it may have been a major thing like giving a significant amount of money to a friend who is in dire need of financial help. I believe God uses these nudges toward generosity to test our faith. Unfortunately, what often happens is that we are so busy, so preoccupied, so concerned with our own well-being that we miss the nudge, the opportunity to be generous, to truly exemplify Jesus. Another problem is our tendency to analyze and rationalize to the extent that we deny the opportunity – nothing more than a way of justifying our inaction. We must be careful not to react like the rich young ruler in Luke 18. Convicted that he may not be on the path to heaven, he asked Jesus, *"What must I do to inherit eternal life?"* Jesus' response was to *"sell everything . . . and follow me."* The young man walked away with a heavy heart *"because he was very wealthy."* He was convicted for a moment, but his fear and greed caused him to rationalize and refuse Jesus' invitation. The next time you are convicted, act. Do something. Make a difference. Be generous.

If you take that first step, even a small one, you have stepped out on the journey of generosity. You have moved from conviction to conversion. Instead of responding like the rich young ruler who chose not to act, we should be like the farmer who found a hidden treasure in a field. In his great joy, he went and sold everything he had and acquired the field.

Generosity is a journey of joy, not a destination. It's a conversion experience that lasts a lifetime. It starts with a conviction but ultimately is a learned character trait that happens as we yield our spirit to the Holy Spirit. At some point along the way, the trait becomes our habit. After numerous convictions and conversion experiences, we make the commitment to not only give but to live generously. We make a living by what we get; we make a LIFE by what we give.

A high-impact LIFE is the journey from success to satisfied significance to total surrender. It's about being all in. Am I there in my personal life? No, and I probably never will be. But every day that I wake, I make it my goal to be a generous steward. I am not perfect, but I am on the journey.

This journey of generosity for me has been – and will continue to be – one of the most life-changing and life-challenging experiences I engage in. Perfect generosity is the capstone to a high-impact LIFE. It is the finish line. At that point, my relationship with God, my relationships with people, my pursuit of excellence, and my concept of stewardship will all have been radically altered and forever changed.

Here are four lessons I have learned on this journey of generosity.

1. *Generosity takes faith.* If our giving isn't large enough to test our faith, our giving isn't large enough.

2. *Generosity needs a plan.* As the old saying goes, plan your work and work your plan. "You should give what you have decided in your heart to give" (2 Corinthians 9:7). For our giving to have the greatest impact, it needs to engage our head with a plan and our heart with a promise.

3. *Generosity requires accountability.* As we become more financially successful, our goal should be to increase our standard of giving, not our standard of living. The only way I have found to combat this malady is to have trusted friends who will hold me accountable to be a faithful steward instead of a selfish owner.

4. *Generosity requires us to ask the hard questions* such as, *how much is enough?* The best decision my wife and I have ever made was to cap our lifestyle and the amount of personal income we received each year from the business. The real question often is not how much is enough, but how much should I be paid to steward the capital God has given me to manage?

Another difficult question is how much should I give? Too often I hear the answer that it's not about the amount; it's about the attitude of your heart. And frankly, this is an excuse for being a stingy giver. Matthew 6:21 tells us, *"For where your treasure is, there your heart will be also."* The amount matters because it is an indication of our heart. The right amount is the amount that moves your heart. It's the amount that forces you to take a risk. It's the amount that stretches your faith. It's the amount that crimps your lifestyle. It's the amount that costs you something. That said, generosity is not governed by the amount given but by the capacity to give. Therefore, a widow's mite means much more to God than a rich person who publicly tips the Lord only to be seen. If it doesn't cost you something, I am not sure it matters to God.

Generosity is not only about what you give but why you're giving. It's a result of *being* (the why) not just *doing* (the what). It's not about just giving because someone asks you to give (doing). It's about spending time with God so that He can influence and direct you in your giving journey (being). Being, knowing God in an intimate way, *and* doing, physically giving, often result in miraculous achievements. Our graphic now includes the principle of Stewarding Capital with its accompanying virtues of Perspective, Integrity, and Generosity.

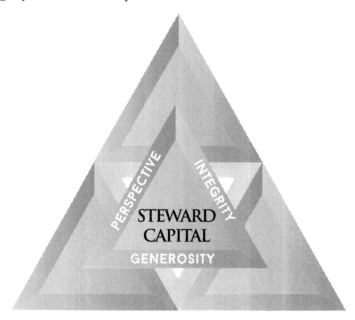

Todd Harper, in his book Abundant, has identified three characteristics of people who model generous living:

Characteristic #1: Generous living is open-hearted. Those who live generously are open-hearted and alert to find people who are struggling, hurting, or in pain. They empathize with those whose world is difficult and they enjoy trying to make it better.

Characteristic #2: Generous living is open-minded. The minds of those who live generously are always thinking about creative ways to bless and encourage others in both great and small ways. They are consciously engaged in their world and the lives of those around them, poised to show generosity to anyone whenever the opportunity presents itself.

Characteristic #3: Generous living is open-handed. The capital of those who live generously are ready to be given gladly whenever a need or an opportunity is discovered. When it is within their power to respond, they relish the privilege to make a difference and bless the life of another – whether friend or stranger. They live out the extreme attitude, "What is mine is yours and you can have it."

In my experience, it has been vividly demonstrated that the key to living a generous life is easy to understand. It is, however, quite difficult to live because of what it requires of us – a radical change in our self-assessment. Paul tells us in Philippians 2:3, "*. . . but with humility of mind regard one another as more important than yourselves*" (NASB). There it is – in just one part of one verse – regard one another as more important than yourself. If we can wholly embrace this radical change in our self-assessment and truly believe that others are more important than ourselves, we will be completely transformed not just into people who are giving generously, but more importantly, into people who are living generously: people who reflect an open-hearted, open-minded, and open-handed life. This achieves maximum Kingdom impact, the high-impact LIFE.

SUMMARY

Stewardship is the careful management of something entrusted to our care. It is an essential part of a high-impact LIFE that we must master if we are going to serve the Master. The essential character quality that drives stewardship is commitment – a commitment to living in such a way that nothing we have, do, or say is ours. It is a commitment to live for Jesus, who was the ultimate standard of commitment for us. He gave His life to give us LIFE and to show us how to live LIFE. Jesus' death is an act of self-emptying love that Christians are explicitly called to imitate, not only with our lives but with all the tangible and intangible assets God has entrusted to our stewardship. In the end, the true measure of our commitment, the true measure of our stewardship, is the degree to which our generosity brings us into closer conformity with Jesus Christ and His death on the cross.

END OF CHAPTER REFLECTION

How can you live more open-hearted, open-minded, and open-handed?

_____

_____

_____

_____

_____

_____

_____

What capital/ideas am I charged to steward?

_____

_____

_____

_____

_____

_____

_____

_____

Notes

Embrace trials and tribulations because they are the tools that God uses to unveil His purpose and plan for your LIFE.

Cheryl Bachelder

CHAPTER 7

CREATED TO FLOURISH

"Wealth consists not in having many possessions but few wants"

Epictetus

O VER THE LAST SIX CHAPTERS WE FOCUSED, on two of the three attributes of living a high-impact LIFE: **loving your purpose** and **living with passion**. A commitment to these two elements is essential before you can succeed at the third attribute, leveraging your platform. Our platform is our vocational calling. It is the work that God has given to each of us to live a LIFE that is honoring and glorifying to Him. If we love our purpose and live with passion, our platform will generate great satisfaction and joy as our work becomes a sacred calling. All of our time, talent, and treasure begin to coalesce around a surrendered LIFE that God can use as His instrument for human flourishing. We will come to understand the power of serving others, pursuing excellence, and being great stewards of God's creation. We will experience shalom, what the Old Testament calls a blessed life.

Shalom, or human flourishing, was fully manifested for a brief period in human history. This period was after the creation of man but before man chose to be his own moral authority. Genesis 2:15-18 lays out this flourishing scenario for us.

"The Lord God took the man and put him in the Garden of Eden to work it and take care of it. And the Lord God commanded the man, 'You are free to eat from any tree in the garden; but you must not eat from the tree of the knowledge of good and evil, for when you eat of it you will surely die.' The Lord God said 'It is not good for the man to be alone. I will make a helper suitable for him.'"

This passage lays out the three essential elements required for flourishing: material provision, relationships, and a purpose for living. The first is material provision. God placed man in the garden to work it and take care of it (verse 15). And the result of work is material provision – food, clothing, and shelter. These physical necessities of life are attained by working, and we call this "economic capital."

The second element is relationships. Seeing that it was not good for the man to be alone, God created a helper (verse 18). We were created to live in community, to live with deep, authentic relationships with our fellow man. Only through community can the common good be promoted; it happens when like-minded people come together to pursue a common cause. This we call "social capital."

The third element is a strong purpose for living, without which man cannot peacefully and successfully live in a free and open society. This purpose includes a moral authority for how we are to live in order to achieve LIFE. In verses 16 and 17 God lays down His first moral boundary in the form of a prohibition: Don't eat of the fruit of that tree, for then you will know the difference between good and evil.

There was purpose both before and after this knowledge, but now the purpose becomes more difficult to achieve. We must understand the difference between good and evil and live accordingly if we are to flourish. The complexities of living in community with market-driven economic transactions, interdependent relationships, private property, and competing interests cannot be beneficially managed without a rule of law, a moral code, a purpose for living for something greater than yourself. This is called "spiritual capital." Adding our three forms of capital to the Impact Framework, it now looks like this.

A high-impact LIFE (or business, family, or church) is the intersection of economic, social, and spiritual capital. In the secular world this intersection is referred to as a "triple bottom line" approach to business. The term has become popular with the secular investing community because they realize that the focus on creating only economic capital can lead to abuses of power and people. A singular focus on economic capital actually impedes flourishing because it often sacrifices relationships (social capital) and morality (spiritual capital) for the sake of maximizing financial gain.

This secular approach to the triple bottom line typically revolves around the triune concepts of people, planet, and profit. While we endorse this movement and understand that it addresses the *who, where,* and *what,* it lacks the crucial fundamental component of why; and it is the why that then determines the how.

> *It is the **why** that then determines the **how**.*

Without a strong moral purpose (a moral code) by which to determine why and how to help people, planet, and profit, the model becomes precarious at best. Most often it loses its way due to the absence of a higher moral authority. A human-centered rule of law is unworkable. If the rule of law is determined by you and me, what happens when we disagree? Unfortunately, might becomes right, relegating us to a twisted golden rule: he who has the gold, rules.

History amply demonstrates the fallacy of this argument. In contrast, William Booth, the founder of the Salvation Army (one of the most renowned organizations for promoting the common good), was often quoted as saying that the Army would "promote the three S's: soup [economic], soap [social], and salvation [spiritual]."

Over the last twenty years, our company has come to fully embrace this triple bottom line approach to LIFE and business. In fact, our company is called "Capital III" because our primary goal in business is to create not only economic capital but social and spiritual capital as well. The philosophy or business model that we employ to ensure that our company creates economic, social, and spiritual capital is called Enterprise Stewardship.

ENTERPRISE STEWARDSHIP

We define an enterprise as "an important or difficult project, especially one requiring boldness and energy." Stewardship is "the trusted management and protection of another's property." It then follows that "enterprise stewardship" is "managing with boldness and energy the important projects God has entrusted to us."

Let's start with what might qualify as an important project. It could it be your business, your church, the nonprofit where you volunteer. It could be your family, your kids, or even yourself. I have come to realize over the years that all of us have various enterprises that must be stewarded, starting with ourselves. As we discover that stewarding our life is the starting point, then the Lord will entrust us with more and more to manage, whether it is a business, a church, a ministry, our family, or some other enterprise. The most thrilling part of embracing a LIFE of stewardship is that it gives each of us a significant part in solving the world's greatest problem: the poverty that is simultaneously economic, social, and spiritual.

CREATING ECONOMIC, SOCIAL, AND SPIRITUAL CAPITAL

Our driving purpose for creating economic, social and spiritual capital is to promote human flourishing. Or in some sense, to eliminate poverty. Let's start this process by understanding the relationship of poverty to wealth to capital.

Poverty is the state of insufficiency, or simply "not having enough." Wealth, on the other hand, is "enough." It is enough of the necessary provisions to provide a life that is capable of flourishing. And capital is "more than enough" or actually, excess wealth – wealth that is above the amount needed for basic provision. Capital is wealth we are willing to invest, to put at risk with the expectation of a greater reward.

Capital is wealth we are willing to invest, to put at risk with the expectation of a greater reward.

It is important to understand that poverty, wealth, and capital are not limited just to defining your economic status but also your social and spiritual status. And all three are required for flourishing. Imagine the three legs of the economic, social, and spiritual capital triangle as spokes of a wheel. If these three spokes aren't in balance, you will have a bumpy journey through life.

If you are lacking in any one of the forms of capital, you are not flourishing. Being rich (economic wealth) without friends (social poverty) is not flourishing. Loving Jesus (spiritual wealth) but having no food (economic poverty) is not flourishing. Being rich (economic wealth) and famous (social wealth) but without great character (spiritual poverty) is not flourishing. To flourish we need economic, social, and spiritual wealth. For those of us fortunate to have excess wealth, whether economic, social, or spiritual, view it as capital to have great impact.

This distinction between wealth and capital is demonstrated in Matthew 25 in the parable of the talents. A master was going on a long journey, so he called in his three stewards and entrusted them with his property. To one he gave five talents; to another, two talents; and to another, one talent. He gave to each according to their ability. Essentially, the master gave each steward "wealth" in the form of gold talents. The steward who had received five talents *"went at once and put his money to work."* So did the steward who had received two. In other words, they took the "wealth" they had been given and *"put [it] to work."* They essentially invested it in a project that required risk. In doing so, they took the wealth they had been entrusted with and converted it to capital. The result was doubling their original investment.

However, the one who had been given only one talent buried it under his tent – taking no risk and receiving no return – because he was afraid to take risk. After a time, the master returned to take an account of how the stewards had invested his wealth. The master was happy with the two stewards who had doubled their shares and said to them, "*Well done, good and faithful [stewards]. You have been faithful with a few things; I will put you in charge of many things. Come and share your master's happiness!*" The master was quite unhappy with the steward who buried his one talent, even to the point of calling him wicked and lazy and taking his wealth and giving it to the stewards who had been faithful.

Here, then, is the question: Are you investing your capital, your "excess wealth" or are you hoarding it in the bottom of your tent?

God has gifted each of us in different ways. Some have been gifted to create financial or economic capital. Others have been gifted in the areas of relationships or social capital. And still others have been gifted in spiritual capital, helping the rest of us on our journey of faith and encouraging us to live lives pleasing to God. As we think about leveraging our platform, it is important to understand how God has designed each of us to fit into the mosaic of human flourishing. Let's look at the three forms of capital and explore what they are, why they are important, and how each of us can leverage them to create greater impact in our world.

ECONOMIC CAPITAL

Economic capital is the material benefit derived from the stewardship of our LIFE (Labor, Influence, Financial capital, Expertise). It is the result of the faithful investment of our time, tribe, treasure, and talent. Until the 1700s, most of the world operated under a traditional economic system. Wealth was measured in the amount of physical assets a person owned, such as land, a dwelling, livestock, grain, etc. This holds true even today for approximately 40 percent of the world that lives on less than three dollars per day. In advanced economies with divisions of labor, free markets, private property, and corporate profits, economic wealth and capital are often held not only in physical assets but in other nonphysical financial assets such as stocks, bonds, options, and cash or currency. Additionally, much wealth today is held in corporations rather than by individuals.

Accumulating wealth in nonphysical assets is beneficial because they are more easily transferred or converted into cash. Highly transferable currency can purchase material possessions or be invested in additional financial assets. It can also be used to support the needs of those less fortunate and can be literally "wired" to the other side of the globe.

Economic capital is important to us because it is required for our basic physical needs. Consequently, it demands a large proportion of our time and is one of the main things that can distract us from having a great relationship with God.

The parable of the talents teaches us about why and how we should create economic capital. First, God expects us to use and steward our abilities. We are not to hide them, squander them, or spend them only on ourselves, because the result will be our downfall. We are to work, take risk, and not be lazy. As a result, God will multiply our efforts. Another lesson this parable hints at is the temptation to get rich quick. Note that the master returned home *after a long time.* Assuming a long time is measured in multiple years, the stewards who doubled their share would have received a reasonable annual return. Proverbs 20:21(TLB) tells us that *"Quick wealth is not a blessing in the end,"* and 21:5 adds, *"Steady plodding brings prosperity; hasty speculation brings poverty."* The creation of economic capital is expected of us, and it is often a long and steady journey.

In addition to providing our basic physical needs, economic capital allows us to fulfill our ultimate purpose and calling in life. The importance of work as it relates to creating economic capital is paramount to a fulfilled LIFE. Work is sacred, not secular, and when we understand that, our work takes on new meaning.

We were created in the image of God, which makes us creative beings. Work is the outlet for our creative nature, giving us dignity and self-worth as it provides the venue to live out our purpose and calling. We have seen this amazing transformation in those we employ inside the prison. Crime and incarceration rob these men of their self-esteem, but when they get a job and begin to work, we see dignity flourish in them from simply doing meaningful work.

Hugh Whelchel, Executive Director of the Institute for Faith, Work & Economics, describes our quest for the purpose, calling, and fulfillment that result from our work.

> *You wake up in the morning hoping your actions will have purpose. You want the work you do during the day to be affirmed, to be directed towards a meaningful end, and to have an impact on the lives of those around you.*
>
> *You want to lie down at night and feel satisfied, content that the work you did was your very best and made a difference in the grand scheme of things. You want the peace of mind, the satisfaction that comes with living out your purpose in the world.*
>
> *You want FULFILLMENT. And you know what? You can find it. Everyone can. You can find fulfillment in many ways, by knowing your place and purpose in your community, your family, your church, and especially in work.*
>
> *. . . Your daily work provides you with the challenges and opportunities to serve God and others. In fact, it's the best way to*

serve others. And service is key — ultimately, work isn't just about your personal fulfillment. It's about serving your neighbors and even complete strangers by using your God-given gifts, talents, and capital to help meet their needs. Your service gives people a glimpse of how things will be when Christ returns and restores creation in full.

There are, of course, times when work may be difficult. Some days you feel the "thorns and thistles," the stress, the burden of your responsibilities more than others. Through it all, work remains a formative activity for finding fulfillment by teaching us about God and ourselves.

Fulfillment can be found in whatever work God places in front of you, regardless of whether it's your dream job or not. When we work hard every day at the work God has given us, it's pleasing to him and way more fulfilling for us.

"So I saw that there is nothing better for a person than to enjoy their work, because that is their lot. For who can bring them to see what will happen after them?" (Ecclesiastes 3:22).

Our work is the foundational component of economic capital, going far beyond merely providing our basic physical needs. Economic capital allows us to create vast forms of social and spiritual capital. Through taxes and charitable contributions we can feed the poor, take care of the sick, maintain our roads, protect our freedom, and fulfill the Great Commission. Economic capital allows us to grow our businesses, hire more people, raise the standard of living for all, and be gospel patrons for causes that ultimately bring glory to God. Economic capital is often the precursor to creating social and spiritual capital.

The final reason to pursue the creation of economic capital is that God will reward us for our faithful stewardship. As we are given more to steward, we will experience a joyful, fulfilled LIFE. The parable of the talents defines our reward for working faithfully: *"You have been faithful with a few things; I will put you in charge of many things. Come and share your master's happiness."* For stewards, the work of managing well and creating additional capital is life giving and rewarding. It is the fruit of our labor, fulfilling the natural longing in our souls. Even more important, it allows us to *"share [our] master's happiness"* as we look forward to hearing *"Well done, good and faithful servant!"*

CREATING ECONOMIC CAPITAL

Two primary economic systems operate in the world today: capitalism and socialism. Capitalism is a decentralized form of economics whereby the main economic drivers are owned, managed, and led by the private marketplace. Several key fundamental factors are essential for capitalism to work properly. These include the rule of law, private property, free and open markets, minimal governmental regulation, and the accumulation of capital for reinvestment in new ideas and businesses. While a great benefit of capitalism is that it moves many people out of extreme poverty, the primary complaint is that it often concentrates wealth in the hands of a few. Socialism, on the other hand, is a centralized system with a strong adherence to the philosophy that markets, production, and distribution should be centralized and controlled by government. Socialism discourages personal property ownership and uses centralized control to redistribute wealth.

Which economic system provides the best opportunities to create economic capital? Since biblical times, private property, markets, and profits have been present in economies. As markets progressed, wealth began to move from land owners and the political elite to the masses in general. This happened as innovation and ideas created enterprises that allowed common people to increase their economic wealth. Capitalism was born. As capitalism took hold, it created wealth for many people, unleashing a work ethic, creativity, and entrepreneurial spirit for millions of people who have subsequently created the greatest wealth in history. China and India alone have raised over 500 million people out of poverty through capitalistic endeavors. In 1970, 76% of the world's poor were in Asia with 11% in Africa. Today, those numbers are essentially switched, with Asia having 15% of the world's poor and Africa 66%.

However, while capitalism has resulted in economic gain for millions of poor people, it has also generated great inequalities in income distribution. Sadly, it has created societies that are focused on individual gain instead of the common good. As the desire to attain greater wealth increases, morality and virtuous business practices have often taken a back seat to greed and unethical practices. David Brooks, an Op-Ed columnist for the New York Times, sums up the problem in a very cogent way.

> In 1976, Daniel Bell published a book called The Cultural Contradictions of Capitalism. Bell argued that capitalism undermines itself because it nurtures a population of ever more self-gratifying consumers. These people may start out as industrious, but they soon get addicted to affluence, spending, credit, and pleasure and stop being the sort of hard workers capitalism requires.

> Bell was right that there's a contradiction at the heart of capitalism, but he got its nature slightly wrong. Affluent, consumerist capitalists still work hard. Just look around.

> The real contradiction of capitalism is that it arouses enormous ambition, but it doesn't help you define where you should focus it. It

doesn't define an end to which you should devote your life. It nurtures the illusion that career and economic success can lead to fulfillment, which is the central illusion of our time.

Capitalism on its own breeds people who are vaguely aware that they are not living the spiritually richest life, who are ill-equipped to know how they might do so, who don't have the time to do so, and who, when they go off to find fulfillment, end up devoting themselves to scattershot causes and light religions.

To survive, capitalism needs to be embedded in a moral culture that sits in tension with it and provides a scale of values based on moral and not monetary grounds. Capitalism, though, is voracious. The personal ambition it arouses is always threatening to blot out the counterculture it requires.

I am fully convinced that the most efficient and effective way to create economic capital is through a free market capitalistic economy, but this only works if the participants accept a moral code that provides the principles and virtues necessary for the system to function in a manner available to all. If we desire to lead the creation of economic capital protected by such a moral code, we must ask difficult but necessary questions to ensure good stewardship of the capital entrusted to our management.

• Is our primary purpose to create wealth for the shareholder at the expense of creating good jobs for our employees with fair pay and excellent benefits?

• Are we challenging our employees to be the best people they can be physically, emotionally, financially, and spiritually?

• Do we pay our vendors timely and treat them as partners in our business?

- Do we treat our customers fairly with a guarantee of quality, timeliness, and a fair price?

- Do we provide fair and accurate returns to our financial shareholders?

Economic capital is essential if we are to flourish. But economic capital, unfettered and left alone as the primary driver of a fulfilled life, will fail if not governed by a moral authority or kept in check by strong authentic relationships. Economic capital is one third of the flourishing equation. Let's look at the second part of the equation: social capital.

CREATING SOCIAL CAPITAL

Social Capital is comprised of the mutual benefits (economic, relational, emotional, political, spiritual, etc.) derived by a group of like-minded people pursuing a common cause. The key driver is relationship. Social capital is the relational wealth that makes communities and organizations function effectively for the common good. Economic capital, including profit maximization and stakeholder wealth, cannot be accomplished long term in the absence of social capital, because ultimately, business cannot be profitably transacted in an environment void of relationships.

Social capital demands mutual trust, common beliefs, shared rules, shared culture, and shared experience, all of which ensure a positive atmosphere and culture for achieving enterprise objectives. In one sense, social capital entails all the things that economic capital can't buy, such as deep and lasting relationships, a commitment to the common good, and a deep concern for the environment that God has given us to steward. Social capital manifests itself in the form of safe communities, good race relations, happy employees, an unpolluted environment, fine art, great music, patriotism, unified families, bipartisan politics, and a genuine love for our fellow human beings.

Perhaps the most compelling reason for the importance of social capital is that it is a foundational component for human flourishing. In Genesis, God created man and declared that it was not good for him to be alone. So, He created woman. God created us to be in relationship and in community. Simply look at communities that have strong relationships and great social capital, and you will see people flourishing. A socially vibrant community is an essential part of who we are and who we become as individuals, families, neighborhoods, churches, and businesses.

God designed various social institutions to create social capital. Let's look closely at four: the family, the church, business, and government.

First, social capital is essential for strong families. Families are, and should be, the primary conveyor of values, religious beliefs, work ethic, political freedom, and an environment where unconditional love is learned. These attributes are passed down because of great relationships between family members.

Second, social capital is essential for vibrant, effective churches that are the primary sustainers and facilitators of a strong moral code, a north star for the fulfillment of our purpose. The fellowship of believers is an integral part of a strong church and a strong community. Being a provider of good works for the common good is a way the church demonstrates its love for Jesus and the community it serves.

Third, social capital is essential in creating trusted businesses. Businesses thrive when there is mutual trust between all stakeholders including customers, vendors, employees, shareholders, and management. Cooperation results in relationships that benefit

Social capital is essential in creating trusted businesses.

the common good. In our business, we often differentiate between regular customers and vendors and those who qualify as "partners." Partners are those vendors or customers with whom we possess great relationships, knowing that if either party needs a favor, the other party will work diligently to help.

Finally, social capital is essential for cities, states, and nations to thrive. Strong cultural and social norms passed down from generation to generation have resulted in an American society that cherishes our individual right to life, liberty, and the pursuit of happiness. It allows freedom of speech and religion and creates entrepreneurial opportunities. It allows us to live in a country with many freedoms because it promotes the concept of individual responsibility and self-governance instead of a top-down dictatorial government with excessive rules and regulations. This results in a society that is safe, educated, and unified, an environment where anyone can become who they desire to be.

Social capital creates a sense of pride and patriotism as well as a desire to assist the rest of the world in times of crisis. America has been revered by the world for our compassion to help in times of war and peace. This statement is frequently attributed to Alexis de Tocqueville in the 1800s: "America is great because she is good, and if America ever ceases to be good, she will cease to be great."

Social capital is not only about the relationship with our fellow man but also the relationship between us and the creation we have been given to steward. The stewardship of our natural capital and the protection of our environment are fundamental to human flourishing. In the end, creating social capital is the responsibility of every human being. Government can mandate rules and regulations but not the hearts of citizens. Businesses can promote ethical principles, but if they don't reside in the heart of the employee, they sound like hollow platitudes. Churches can promote the commandment to love your neighbor as yourself, but if the parishioner does not have love in his heart, he will not love his neighbor. God created us for relationship, and the responsibility to create social capital lies squarely with each of us as individuals.

My friend Cheryl Bachelder's platform story is like a roller-coaster ride that weaves beautifully together in the creation of all three capitals.

As a young adult, I did not know and understand my God-given purpose, passion, and platform. I needed preparation, and my family was a remarkable influence for that time. My parents raised their four children with a sound education, a Midwestern work ethic, and a strong foundation of faith. My grandmothers were also significant teachers of faith lessons. One lesson I remember well was my paternal grandmother reminding me that anxiety is not from God — and then she would quote Scripture about how God clothed the lilies of the field — would He not also take care of me?

I accepted Christ in my eighth-grade confirmation class and dedicated my life to Him in front of the entire church congregation. My life verse as a young adult was "Seek first the kingdom of God and his righteousness, and all these things will be added to you" (Matthew 6:33, ESV).

This faith foundation served me well through college and my twenties. I read my Bible, journaled, and went to church — knowing that this would always be part of my life. I married young, and together Chris and I pursued careers and built our family, having two beautiful daughters. As I look back on that time, I'm rather amazed at the intensity of those years. There was so much to do, to plan, to achieve, to accomplish. At one point, I realized that pounding headaches had become my daily norm. All this doing and accomplishing was exhausting – and I wasn't really sure what the point of it all was. Were any of us thriving? Were we honoring God with stewardship and excellence? Or were we racing to some imaginary finish line where we would skid into heaven sideways – exhausted by our efforts to please God?

When our children were young, Chris and I began to go deeper in our Bible study. We enrolled in a three-year discipleship class where we read and studied the entire Bible, Old and New Testament. A few years later I came across a seminal book called Your Work Matters to God – and this gave me a fresh understanding of how God sees work and how it can be a way to serve and honor Him with our lives. Then Chris and I participated in the Henry Blackaby study, Experiencing God, and discovered that our "job" was to look where God is working – and simply join him there. We didn't have to strive and search so hard; we needed to slow down, look to see where God had a plan, and offer to help Him accomplish that plan.

Both Chris and I love to learn, so study became the primary expression of our faith in this stage. Perhaps we thought study was the path to purpose and peace. But eventually, even study becomes a race to an imaginary finish line. Can we ever learn all we need to know to best serve our Heavenly Father?

It was time to understand God's view of purpose. Up until now, we would have said we were blessed and thriving despite the exhaustion.

But God brought us to the most important lessons in our lives through trials and tribulations. I now refer to these as the "treasures" God used to fortify our walk with Him.

First treasure? I was diagnosed with stage I breast cancer at the age of 45, when our daughters were 10 and 15. It was frightening and confusing. Were we not faithfully doing all we could for God? Wouldn't He honor our efforts with a long, blessed life? Why would He cut short our time with one another — our love for each other? Looking back, my response was all about me.

While sorting through treatment plans and all these faith questions, we met our second treasure. I was fired from the pinnacle job of my career, president of KFC restaurants. This was my platform — the way I would model leadership as a follower of Christ. This was my calling — and I had hoped to do it well. But after a short period of negative sales in a high-pressure public company, I was humbled, even humiliated, to be a newspaper headline — "CEO replaced at KFC."

Was I not faithfully doing what I had promised God? Why would He cut short my platform in the marketplace? Why would He allow this devastation of my confidence and my understanding of my calling? Looking back, it was another "all about me" response.

God used the treasures of trials to bring me totally to my knees and to a surrendered position — face down on the pavement — begging for His mercy and grace. During this time I read The Purpose-Driven Life by Rick Warren. I only needed to find the life changing words on page 1 of Chapter 1. He begins by raising the question, what is the purpose of your life? Look at what he says in all caps:

IT'S NOT ABOUT YOU. The purpose of your life is far greater than your own personal fulfillment, your peace of mind, or even your happiness. It is far greater than your family, your career, or even your wildest dreams and ambitions. If you want to know why you were placed on this planet, you must begin with God. You were born by his purpose and for his purpose.

As I processed these important words over the next few years, God revealed exactly what He was working on and how I could serve HIS purpose while on this earth. It was a revelation of His incredible mercy and grace. It was a revelation of His calling on my life. It was proof of His redeeming death on the cross.

My preparatory years had given me a tremendous insight into the strengths and weaknesses of leaders in large corporations. I had seen a few "gems" and a lot of ordinary "rocks." I had seen the leadership traits that led people to flourish and perform their best work. And I had seen the spirit-crushing effect of self-absorbed leaders on an organization.

God has given us His model for leadership – in the life of His son, Jesus Christ. And it is the most counterintuitive and effective approach to reaching the hearts and minds of human beings. So what was God up to? He wanted to see a movement of leaders who are bold enough to serve Him in the marketplace.

The marching orders came to me in this one sentence in the foreword of a book entitled, On Moral Business. Dr. Max Stackhouse describes how so many of our institutions are failing society; then he lays out this challenge: "Increasingly, business leaders may be the stewards of civilization."

With this enriched perspective of God's worldview, my personal passion and purpose became: to inspire purpose-driven leaders to exhibit confidence and character in all aspects of their lives. I was to teach the principles of servant leadership in the secular, public-company environment. My life verse for this stage came from Philippians 2:3, "Do nothing from selfish ambition or conceit but, in humility, count others more significant than yourselves" (ESV).

Shortly after this I was asked to serve as CEO of Popeyes, a global restaurant chain selling flavorful chicken and delicious biscuits. This was the platform God provided for me to join Him in His purpose. I would steward this organization to understand that servant leadership was the path to honoring God and achieving superior performance results. Because God knew that this approach would create a place where human beings would thrive and give their very best – because they were loved, cared for, and grown in capability and character.

This one leadership story alone would not change the course of history – but it would become one case study for the world to consider. In 2015, the story was told in the book Dare to Serve: how to drive superior results by serving others. It is a secular book, built on the principles of Christ. Thousands of people in public and private corporations have been challenged to consider God's leadership philosophy. And many more are now writing and telling the story of servant leadership's impact on their organizations. The servant leadership movement has been revived – and the evidence is compelling. This is how God has moved in the marketplace. And I have been blessed to be a small part of His purposes.

God prepared me diligently through family, life experiences, and faith. God revealed HIS purposes and His plans to me, largely through trials and tribulations. And finally, God redeemed all the misguided things I did early in my life and work and allowed me to work for Him, on His platform, and for His purposes.

HIGH IMPACT HABIT
Embrace trials and tribulations because they are the tools that God uses to unveil His purpose and plan for your LIFE.

To God be the glory for the things HE has done!

The creation of social capital is summed up by two commandments: Love the Lord your God with all your heart, soul, and mind and love your neighbor as yourself. Christians and non-Christians alike understand the command to love your neighbor. What we often overlook, however, is the commandment to love the Lord your God with all your heart, soul, and mind. It is critical that we start with the first commandment because it is the one that changes our hearts and allows us to love others, even those we really don't want to love.

Romans 13:8 says, "*Owe no one anything except to love one another, for he who loves another has fulfilled the law*" (NKJV). To owe no financial debt is to be financially free, a wise position for which to strive. But there is a kind of debt we should never seek to escape: the debt of genuine love for our family, friends, and neighbors. To stop loving others would mean to live only for ourselves. Genuine love binds us together. It allows us to view the world differently. It is inexhaustible. It also changes the questions we ask in life from "Is it good for me?" to "Is it good for my neighbor?" When my neighbor gets the promotion I was seeking, or the new car I wanted, I can genuinely rejoice in their accomplishment when I have loved them as myself.

Social capital is not created by institutionalized mandates but by the selfless actions of individuals seeking to further the common good. Individual self-governance and responsibility that stir the soul to serve others instead of self will result in the abundant creation of social capital. We must take on the mantle of faithful stewards, promoting the common good by promoting and supporting the key institutions in our society.

We must promote and support family because it is the primary building block of society. It is the most effective and efficient enterprise for creating economic, social, and spiritual capital. It is also responsible for sustaining the human race through procreation. It is the sustainer of moral values and is the place where love is best taught, caught and given.

We should be ardent supporters of vibrant churches as the place where we learn to love our neighbor as ourselves. It is the vehicle God has given us to promote truth, faith, and character. It is where we come together to worship, be taught, fellowship, and honor God.

We must have influence in the marketplace, because this is a tremendous platform for us to demonstrate to the world that social capital can make a difference. Business will only thrive in an environment where there is strong social and spiritual capital. Without social capital, economic capital cannot be maintained, because the marketplace is ultimately based on trust and relationships. Without spiritual capital, unethical practices prevail. As Christian business leaders, we should have a line of potential employees standing at our front door desiring to work for our companies because we are the best place to work. We should value our stakeholders by serving them in extraordinary ways.

Finally, we should be active in the governance of our communities, state, and nation. Government exists to protect our social and spiritual capital, not create it. Government's primary role is to defend our right to life, liberty, and the pursuit of happiness. As such, it plays a critical role in creating a state that allows each of us to exercise our individual rights to create and enjoy economic, social, and spiritual capital. As citizens, we must maintain our responsibilities to our fellow citizens through individual self-governance. If we fail to do so, government will step in at the cost of our freedoms.

God established institutions to promote and encourage the creation of social capital and culture. The family is the primary perpetuator of social capital, the church is the primary promoter of spiritual capital, business is the primary provider of economic capital, and government is the protector of the freedoms that allow us to enjoy all three forms of capital. Remember, the ultimate sources of social capital are individuals who have been transformed by the understanding that their purpose in life is to honor God and to exhibit it by loving their neighbors as themselves.

CREATING SPIRITUAL CAPITAL

The term spiritual capital has gained traction over the last twenty years as capitalism has created great wealth – often at the expense of human rights, environmental abuse, religious intolerance, and political domination. During this time, we have seen Enron, the tech bubble, and the financial crisis of 2008 as examples of capitalism gone awry. Consequently, there has been increasing discussion related to the morality of economic and social theory.

The most widely accepted definitions of spiritual capital describe it as the quantified value of spiritual beliefs and practices held by individuals, groups, and society. My problem with most definitions of spiritual capital is that while they define the desired moral outcomes – and I agree with many of them – they fail to address the source of the morality other than to say it is spiritual in nature. Declaring that a moral code is essential does not answer the question of its basis or source. This is critical because it ultimately determines the way one creates spiritual capital.

While not necessarily identifying it as spiritual capital, the world is acutely aware of the need for a strong moral code. In 1998, an independent group of heads of state from around the world issued the Universal Declaration of Human Responsibilities, a statement later considered by the United Nations. One paragraph reads:

> *No person, no group, no organization, no state, no army or police stands above good and evil; all are subject to ethical standards. Everyone has a responsibility to promote good and to avoid evil in all things.*

That is all fine and good. But tell me who defines good and evil. Some apologists have tackled the morality issue as it relates to spiritual capital. One of them is Ravi Zacharias, and based on his work, I propose three primary options as the basis of a moral code.

The first option is a heteronomous approach: you are "subject to another's law" – a government or other institution determines the moral code. In a dictatorship, the law is determined by the dictator; in a democracy, it is determined by the will of the people. It is relative in nature in that it changes with the dictator or the desires of the majority.

A second option is an autonomous approach: the law is "subject to man's own choice." The individual becomes the supreme lawmaker when determining the moral code. As with the heteronomous approach, it is relative in nature in that we as individuals determine what is right and wrong.

A third option, and my choice, is the theonomous approach: the moral code is "subject to God's law." Unlike the others, it is absolute because it comes from the ultimate authority. This is an absolutist approach, which tends to be unpopular in our me-centered world. None of us want to be confined to someone else's moral authority, but moral relativity is essentially no moral code at all. Without moral absolutes, anything goes. Might is right. I'm okay, but you're not okay. The history of human atrocities over the past few decades is enough to demonstrate the severe limitations of human relativism.

I define spiritual capital as the moral code by which one's life is based on truth (in God's Word), faith (in Jesus Christ), and character (Obedience to God's will) as defined in _____ God's holy word. Spiritual capital is important because it answers the why question. Only when we understand _____ that we have been transformed by the saving grace of Jesus Christ and the indwelling power of the Holy Spirit can we grasp the amazing opportunities we have to impact the world. It changes our focus from serving self to honoring God.

Spiritual capital is important because it answers the why question.

A second reason Spiritual capital is essential is that it is the moral code by which we create economic and social capital. Our country has become divided over two basic metaphysical philosophies that drive the way we think and act: the sacred versus the secular, the autonomous versus the theonomous, the human-centered way versus God's way. As we have removed God from our culture, our pursuit of loving our neighbor as ourselves has become almost extinct. The result is a society that has become intolerant, base, and self-serving with very little appetite for promoting the common good. Rancor, name calling, and demagoguery in the cowardly form of tweeting and twittering have become standard operating procedures.

Capitalism without God and a theocentric moral code results in greed, and its fruit includes labor abuse, price fixing, Wall Street scandals, and a host of other economic maladies. However, capitalism with a theocentric moral code results in generosity. It uses the profits for the common good instead of self. In the same way, government without God results in totalitarianism under the thumb of a political class that seeks to further their own careers instead of serving their constituents. Government with God results in political freedom because it drives the community to pursue the common good as its people live under the mandate to love neighbor as self.

Society requires a moral code to function. When God is taken out of the culture, a moral vacuum arises that must be replaced by alternative rules. Too often, God gets replaced by government. As a result, instead of a society whose moral code is dictated by self-governed individuals seeking to love their neighbor as themselves, we have a society of self-seeking citizens who promulgate rules to serve their own self interests. As God-given ethics are replaced with man-made rules and regulations, the ultimate price is a loss of economic and political freedoms.

Historically, countries often progress from a theonomous culture, where each individual self-governs with virtues focused on the common good, to a heterogeneous culture, where the moral code is dictated by government, to an autonomous culture, where self-governance is replaced by self-indulgence. This leads to a breakdown of economic and social order. We clearly see this progression in action in the histories of Rome in the 200s, Germany in the 1930s, Russia in the 1980s, and America today.

Spiritual capital is essential if we are to remain economically, politically, and spiritually free. To our Founding Fathers it was obvious, "self-evident," that a democratic republic could only be perpetuated by the self-governed. To this end, the founders fundamentally believed that the ability to govern ourselves rests with our individual and collective virtue, in other words, a strong moral code.

Washington, Franklin, and Jefferson expressed the sentiment that only a virtuous people can maintain a free society. John Adams gives us an example of this thinking in his letter to the officers of the Massachusetts First Brigade in October of 1798: "We have no government armed with power capable of contending with human passions unbridled by morality and religion ... Our Constitution was made only for a moral and religious people. It is wholly inadequate to the government of any other."

Over the course of Western civilization, Christianity has provided the moral foundation on which societies have been built. It gave believers and nonbelievers alike a framework for understanding right and wrong that went beyond personal feelings. When we look at moral culture today, it closely resembles that of ancient Israel during the time of Judges: " . . . *everyone did what was right in his own eyes*" (Judges 21:25, NASB). Today, the idea of virtue both individually and corporately seems to be lost, and the impact on our society is being felt from the boardrooms on Wall Street to the streets of Chicago. God calls His people to be a virtuous people living lives of good character, which in turn has the potential of lifting society as a whole. Scripture teaches that virtue includes the characteristics of goodwill, patience, tolerance, kindness, respect, humility, gratitude, courage, honor, industry, honesty, chastity, and fidelity. The Founding Fathers understood that these principles are the cornerstones for both individual and societal governance. If we are to make a difference, we need to once again teach virtue to God's people and model it to a lost nation.

"*Finally, brothers and sisters, whatever is true, whatever is noble, whatever is right, whatever is pure, whatever is lovely, whatever is admirable – if anything is excellent or praiseworthy – think about such things. Whatever you have learned or received or heard from me, or seen in me – put it into practice. And the God of peace will be with you*"
-Philippians 4:8-9

Spiritual capital is produced by pursuing the virtues of truth, faith, and character. We must know truth found in Scripture. If we read it, meditate on it, memorize it, and pursue it with all our heart, mind, and soul, we will know the truth and the truth will set us free. We must believe by faith, because without faith, it is impossible to please God. Remember that faith is the fuel that turns knowing into doing. Therefore, believe that Jesus is who He said He was, and believe that you can be transformed by the work of the Holy Spirit in your daily life.

Finally, we must live with character. As it says in James 1:22 (ESV), "*But be doers of the word, and not hearers only, deceiving yourselves.*" John 14:21 says "*Whoever has my commands and obeys them, he is the one who loves me. He who loves me will be loved by my Father, and I too will love him and show myself to him*" (NIV, 1984). We are to live obedient lives that are holy and pleasing to God. That is how we honor God in all we do.

SUMMARY

Flourishing requires the creation of economic, social, and spiritual wealth. For those of us who have chosen to live as stewards instead of owners, our primary challenge is to always reinvest our excess wealth – our economic, social and spiritual capital – back into projects and people to further God's kingdom here on earth. The following table summarizes the three forms of capital along with the purpose, the driver, the currency, and the fulfillment of the biblical mandate of each.

	ECONOMIC	SOCIAL	SPIRITUAL
PURPOSE	MATERIAL PROVISION	COMMON GOOD	FREEDOM (TRUTH)
DRIVER	WORK	TIME	FAITH
CURRENCY	VALUE CREATION	RELATIONSHIPS	CHARACTER
BIBLICAL MANDATE	GREAT CALLING	GREAT COMMANDMENT	GREAT COMMISSION

Are we investing our work, time, and faith to create economic principle, social relationships, and spiritual character to impact the world? Or are we hoarding our excess wealth, like the rich young ruler, by building bigger barns? One choice leads to sharing the Master's happiness for eternity; the other leads to destruction.

Let's take a look at our Impact Framework that now includes the creation of economic, social, and spiritual capital.

Are you leveraging your platform? What vocation, career, and job has God called you to? Are you leveraging it in a way that is pleasing and honoring to Him? I am fully convinced that God cares not only about what you do, but He cares very much about how you do it. What we do, our platform, should be centered on our natural God-given talents. Whether we are butchers, bakers, or candlestick makers, our work is sacred. And because our work is sacred, it's not just about creating economic capital; it is about using our platform to create great relationships (social capital) so that we can have a significant spiritual impact (spiritual capital) with those whom we know and love. Love your purpose, live with passion, and you will enjoy a highly-leveraged platform.

END OF CHAPTER REFLECTION

How am I investing my capital (work, time, etc.)?

_____

_____

_____

_____

_____

_____

Using the High Impact Model, what virtues am I excelling at?
What Virtues are causing me to struggle?

_____

_____

_____

_____

_____

_____

_____

_____

Notes

Practice:
God first,
Others second,
and I'm Third.

Joe White

CHAPTER 8

HIGH IMPACT LIFE

"Do what you can, with what you have, where you are."
Theodore Roosevelt

WHAT, THEN, IS THE PURPOSE IN striving to live a high-impact LIFE? It is to honor God and enjoy Him forever. And this will result in flourishing here on earth and in eternity. This journey is neither easy nor necessarily comfortable, but it is fulfilling beyond our imagination. We will experience the utter fear of stepping out in great faith to the absolute exhilaration of seeing miracles occur. I would like to conclude our journey together by recapping what we have learned and challenging you to take the next steps. As we enter this last chapter, let me review our walk through the Impact Framework in our quest for a high-impact LIFE.

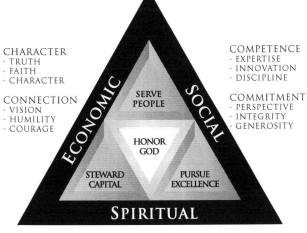

At the center of our high impact model lies our purpose in life, which is to honor God. We honor God by living out the virtues of truth, faith, and character.

This purpose to honor God then determines our new God-pleasing passions of serving people, pursuing excellence, and stewarding capital (gray triangles). Each of these three principles contains three key virtues that will allow us to live out that principle in our lives.

To serve people (connection) we must exercise vision, humility, and courage.

To pursue excellence (competence) we must pursue expertise, innovation and discipline.

To steward capital (commitment) we must have perspective, integrity, and generosity.

When we invest our life by loving our purpose and living with passion, it results in a leveraged platform that creates economic, social, and spiritual capital (a high-impact LIFE). Our purpose in life determines our vocation or calling. Our passion in life determines our career, which should align with our natural God-given talents. And our platform is the current job we work that allows us to live out our purpose and passion for others to see. Here is what it looks like in my life. My purpose (vocational calling) is to honor God as a Christ-centered entrepreneur. My passion (career path) is to use my gifts in business and live them out as an entrepreneur. And my platform (job) has included being a farm kid, a banker, and an entrepreneur. My purpose determined my vocation or calling. My passion determined my career. My platform is my current job. It is imperative to understand that the level of our satisfaction and contentment in life depends on the extent to which we have determined our purpose or vocation first, fleshed out our passions that shape our career path, and then pursued the job that allows us to fulfill our purpose. When we have our vocation (purpose), career (passions), and job (platform) in good alignment, we have positioned ourselves to flourish. That is our ultimate goal. A high-impact LIFE is a life of flourishing and being fruitful. Psalm 92:12 says: "*The righteous flourish like the palm tree, and grow like a cedar in Lebanon. They are planted in the house of the Lord; they flourish in the courts of our God. They still bear fruit in old age*" (ESV). This flourishing and bearing fruit are the two key components of a high-impact LIFE.

Dr. Anne Bradley, Vice President of Economic Initiatives at the Institute for Faith, Work, and Economics, eloquently describes flourishing in her blog post on the subject.

> *There is a universal longing, a desire transcending tribe, tongue, and nation that sits at the core of every human heart. It's a desire for thriving. For blessedness. For fullness of life. For flourishing. Creation as God intended it was in a state of flourishing. Adam and Eve walked in right relationship with God. Everything was as it was supposed to be.*
>
> *Then humanity fell into sin, and God has been calling Christians to work towards reweaving flourishing ever since. Flourishing begins with the work of redemption God undertakes in our souls. He restores us to right relationship with him. We're all in need of a little restoration. When we figure out what God made us for and how we fit into his big picture of restoration, that's when we truly flourish.*
>
> *It doesn't end there, though. Flourishing is about more than our personal redemption or finding our calling. Knowing God is glorified when his creation flourishes, we work for the flourishing of others out*

of gratitude and a desire to spread his glory throughout the earth.

When we serve other people with our God-given gifts, talents, time and capital, we help them flourish.

What does flourishing look like, then? It's when the wilderness becomes fruitful. It's when justice dwells. It's when righteousness abides. It's when people live peacefully. Flourishing is happiness. It's joy. It's a fullness of life. It's wholeness. It's abundance. Flourishing seeks the welfare of the city. It promotes the common good. It radiates God's Kingdom on earth.

Flourishing is a thriving farm. It's a booming city. It's a cure for disease. It's a new technology. It's a beautiful song. It's a vibrant street mural. It's a loving family. It's a fun friendship. It's a deep relationship with God. It's living as an image bearer of our Creator.

Flourishing means becoming everything we were created to be.

Finally, although we are called to bring about ever higher levels of flourishing, we know in the end we're merely giving a glimpse of the restoration that is to come when God ushers in the New Heavens and the New Earth. Flourishing in this life is inevitably incomplete because of God's ongoing mission in the world.

Full flourishing will only be realized with the second coming of Christ and the consummation of his kingdom. It's what we hope for, what each of us longs for deep in our hearts.

In the meantime, we've got work to do. Until he returns, God keeps calling us to do our part in bringing about flourishing for the world.

For people to flourish, they must have adequate material possessions (food, clothing, and shelter); close relationships with their family, friends, and community; a purpose for living that results in a deeply rooted moral code that allows them to live righteously. Flourishing requires economic, social, and spiritual capital.

The second part of a high-impact LIFE is that we bear fruit. Our pursuit of flourishing is not merely for the betterment of our own lives but for the overall common good. In bearing fruit, we are living out the commandment to love our neighbor as ourself. Remember, poverty is having too little, wealth is having enough, and capital is investing our excess wealth to create great eternal impact. This means that for those of us who have been fortunate enough to have capital, it is our responsibility to reinvest it for the purpose of helping others flourish. This is bearing fruit.

> *Poverty is having too little, wealth is having enough, and capital is investing our excess wealth to create great eternal impact.*

The fruit we bear can be the economic capital we create through our efforts in the marketplace. It can be the social capital we create by promoting great relationships in our families, communities, or with the environment in which we live. And it can be spiritual capital in the form of living by God's moral code, a LIFE of trusting in Jesus and being obedient to God's word. When I think of bearing fruit, one of the first examples that comes to mind is the story of Kanakuk Kamps. This brief description from its president, Joe White, is filled with the reinvestment of economic and social capital in the creation of spiritual capital.

> *Kanakuk Kamps is 92 years old. For 92 years, Kanakuk has been a blessed placed. Certainly not flawless, but very blessed. Around 75,000 staff and over half-a-million kids in those 92 years have been impacted for God's kingdom. When you get that many people under one roof, everything is not going to be perfect, but by the grace of God our staff*

has done exceptionally well at carrying out our purpose statement: "Developing dynamic Christian leaders through life-changing experiences, Godly relationships, and spiritual training." This is our calling: to develop men and women who will lead on university campuses in dormitories, athletics, fraternities, and sororities; who will lead in their professional life in business circles and church circles and parachurch circles and missionary circles; men and woman who will be courageous enough to lead boldly as Christian leaders. We understand that they will not always be popular or politically correct, but they will be biblical, and their lives will blaze with purpose and satisfaction as they go all out for Christ. For ten years I spoke at various events for Bill McCartney, former national championship coach of Colorado University and founder of Promise Keepers Ministries. I distinctly remember a tribute banquet I spoke at. I asked one of his national championship players, "How did Bill McCartney win?" He answered, "He believed in us until we believed in ourselves." That statement is my mantra for organizational leadership. To speak. To believe. To have faith in our staff and campers and to keep doing it until they believe in themselves. Most young men have never had a dad or a coach affirm them in a visionary way, giving a positive view of who they see the young man becoming. This is a huge problem in America. The successful coach (i.e., the successful leader) must have the vision to see a goofy seventh grade young man who will be a champion when he is a twelfth grader. A successful coach must see the nineteen-year-old freshman who will be a team leader when he is a senior. Across the stage at Kanakuk, we try to see the future man in a kid at age seven. These seven-, nine-, thirteen-year-old young men and women will be the godly leaders of tomorrow who will make a difference in their home and business for the sake of Christ. They are the next generation. One goal of the football camp I run every summer is to call every camper's name ten times a day — with a word of encouragement. Think of it, every young man hearing his name and something positive about himself ten times a day! This small habit transforms their potential as a person and an athlete. I train my staff to be diligent at catching our campers in the act of doing something good and then affirming the mess out of them. I truly believe that developing leaders is ten percent direction and ninety percent encouragement. This is the art of speaking life into a young man or a young woman, and I've seen this change countless young lives. From a top-to-bottom view of Kanakuk, our vision statement covers a broad context. It says, "To evangelize the next generation to reach the world for Christ." Simply, the two key factors are Christ and the next generation. We keep it simple. This vision statement allows our purpose statement to have a broader and deeper reach. We are not just developing Christian leaders who have eyes for the saved world, but also for the lost world. Our entire nation and the entire world matter to God. Our goal is to reach both. By the grace of God we have been blessed to develop an inner-city ministry over the last 45-50 years (Kids Across America). KAA has reached about 135,000 urban kids in our Kamps. Kanakuk has developed an international ministry that started in Haiti and now spans 40 nations, all to God's glory. We have helped build an organization called Cross International that impacts roughly 800,000 kids around the world. To ensure the continuation of our reach, we are developing leaders with a vision and passion for the urban world. The first step is to help our kids get their eyes off themselves and onto God and others. Our motto is I'm Third, based on Matthew 22:37, where Jesus said, "Love the Lord your God, and love others as yourself." We call that, I'm Third. I'm Third is the view for building a kid who wants to be a next-generation leader and evangelize and equip generations to follow. Scripture tells us that if you put God first, others second, and yourself third, your life won't be all about serving yourself and meeting your own needs. This is a change of heart, not looking for what God can do for you, but looking for what God can do through you to serve and help reach the unreached people that He loves. As a leader you must recognize that vision and mission statements are worthless unless the leaders from the top down – the CEO, CFO, mid-level managers, maintenance personnel, everybody) have the same heartbeat. When every person believes in the vision and purpose of the organization, it brings your vision to life. At Kanakuk, we are thrilled with the buy-in from our staff. But we never stop striving, because we are trying to reach the world for Christ. Our whole team is highly committed to excellence because they believe in our vision. Every summer, our team – from the top down – puts in seven-day weeks at roughly sixteen hours a day – because they are serious about the vision. This extreme buy-in can occur only if we are serious about developing next-generation leaders. Our passion is a reflection of the passion our savior demonstrated when he carried the cross out of the city up to Golgotha, the hill where he was crucified. Jesus accomplished this because He is passionate about His purpose. To imitate Christ in this requires incredible effort and dedication toward the task that God has called us to do today. Today matters. When a lost camper comes through our gates, it breaks our heart. When a hurting kid comes through our gates, it breaks our heart. When we have a broken heart for the lost, we feel their pain and we try to reach them for the Lord. By the grace of God, we have served many kids and staff around the world for numerous years, and the beautiful thing is that no single person on our team takes credit for this win. All of the combined effort of the team has been to serve with the I'm Third philosophy. Our staff bleeds this philosophy, and I am so impressed with them for so many reasons. We've seen the I'm Third philosophy transform the

HIGH IMPACT HABIT

Practicing God first, others second, and I'm Third.

lives of friends, families, and people all over the world.

If we, like Joe, are to experience this life of flourishing and bearing fruit, we must answer the three questions that have been the foundation of this entire book.

1. *Am I loving my purpose?* Do I understand that I must exchange my pursuit of self for the pursuit of God as the center of my universe? This means moving from success to surrender. It requires, as Scott Rodin describes in The Steward's Journey, that I become a steward leader of no reputation, meaning that I don't need to wait to be appointed to an official stewardship role. I can be an anointed steward before being an appointed steward.

2. *Am I living with passion?* Do I understand I am moving from my old life of pursuing pride, pleasure, and possessions to a new LIFE of passionately pursuing service, excellence, and stewardship?

3. *Am I leveraging my platform?* Am I using all my LIFE – my labor, my influence, my financial capital, and my expertise – to create economic, social, and spiritual capital? Is the focus of all of this, all of my LIFE, to create human flourishing and impact the world for Jesus?

LIFE is a journey. We can choose a life in pursuit of success or we can choose a LIFE in pursuit of surrender. One is self-seeking, the other selfless. One is troubled, the other, joyful. One is a wide road, the other is narrow. One is transactional, the other is transformational. One is temporal, the other, eternal. Unfortunately, I didn't choose the surrendered road until I was fifty. But it doesn't matter when the transformation happens; it just needs to happen.

CHALLENGE

At the age of forty I realized that although I had become successful, I was neither surrendered nor satisfied. Over the next ten years I often moved two steps forward and one step back. I soon discovered that the pursuit of a high-impact LIFE was a journey and not an instantaneous conversion. I am still on the journey and have a lot to learn. I want to encourage you to take this journey with me, beginning with a simple step of faith, asking God to show you what He wants you to know (truth), believe (faith), and do (character). It starts with a conviction that something needs to change and a commitment to begin the journey.

To begin, you need to wrestle with the following questions until you are ready to move forward.

• Do you want to take hold of LIFE that is truly LIFE?

_____

_____

• Do you want to make a difference?

_____

_____

• Do you want to lay up treasure for yourself in heaven?

_____

_____

• Do you want to live a LIFE of stewardship?

_____

_____

• Do you want to be blessed and live a life of flourishing not only for yourself but for those you care deeply about?

_____

_____

This journey is vividly described by Jeremiah in chapter 17:5-8. *"This is what the Lord says: Cursed is the one who trusts in man, who draws strength from mere flesh and whose heart turns away from the Lord. That person will be like a bush in the wastelands; they will not see prosperity when it comes. They will dwell in the parched places of the desert, in a salt land where no one lives. But blessed is the one who trusts in the Lord, whose confidence is in him. They will be like a tree planted by the water that sends out its roots by the stream. It does not fear when heat comes; its leaves are always green. It has no worries in a year of drought and never fails to bear fruit."*

If you want to live a high-impact LIFE, then commit today to honor God by surrendering all that you are, all that you have, and all that you might be so that you can serve people, pursue excellence, and steward the vast God-given capital at your disposal. The result will be a little bit of heaven here on earth that we call human flourishing. Can you imagine the great impact?

END OF CHAPTER REFLECTION

Am I using all my LIFE – my labor, my influence, my financial capital, and my expertise – to create economic, social, and spiritual capital?

_____

_____

Labor

_____

Influence

_____

Financial Capital

_____

Expertise

_____

How can I be a better steward?

_____

_____

_____

_____

_____

Notes

_____

_____

_____

_____

_____

_____

_____

_____

_____

_____

_____

_____

_____

_____

_____

_____

_____

Commit today to Honor God by surrendering all that you are, all that you have, & all that you might be.

Pete Ochs

SCRIPTURE ANNOTATIONS

These Scriptures are in the order they appear in the book All are taken from the 2011 NIV unless otherwise noted.

CHAPTER 1. IF SUCCESS DOESN'T BRING SATISFACTION, THEN WHAT DOES?

1. *1 John 2:15-16, NIV 1984. "Do not love the world or anything in the world . . . for everything in the world, the cravings of sinful man, the lust of his eyes and the boasting of what he has and does, comes not from the Father but from the world."*

CHAPTER 2. IT'S ALL ABOUT HAVING THE RIGHT WHY

2. *Genesis 3:5. "For God knows that when you eat from it your eyes will be opened, and you will be like God, knowing good and evil."*

3. *Isaiah 43:7. "everyone who is called by my name, whom I created for my glory, whom I formed and made."*

4. *1 Corinthians 10:31. "So whether you eat or drink or whatever you do, do it all for the glory of God."*

5. *Matthew 5:16. "In the same way, let your light shine before others, that they may see your good deeds and glorify your Father in heaven."*

6. *2 Corinthians 5:17, NIV 1984. "Therefore, if anyone is in*

Christ, he is a new creation; the old has gone, the new has come!"

7.   Galatians 2:20. *"I have been crucified with Christ and I no longer live, but Christ lives in me. The life I now live in the body, I live by faith in the Son of God, who loved me and gave himself for me."*

8.   Matthew 20:28, ESV. *"Even as the Son of Man came not to be served but to serve, and to give his life as a ransom for many."*

9.   1 Chronicles 29:11-12, TLB. *". . . Everything in the heavens and the earth is yours, O Lord, and this is your kingdom. We adore you as being in control of everything. Riches and honor come from you alone, and you are the ruler of all mankind; your hand controls power and might, and it is at your discretion that men are made great and given strength."*

10.   Psalm 139:14. *"I praise you because I am fearfully and wonderfully made; your works are wonderful, I know that full well."*

11.   Matthew 25:14-30. *Parable of the Sower.*

12.   2 Timothy 1:7, NIV 1984. *"God did not give us a spirit of timidity, but a spirit of power, of love and of self-discipline.*

CHAPTER 3. FINDING MY ULTIMATE PURPOSE - HONOR GOD

13.   John 15:5, NIV 1984. *"I am the vine; you are the branches. If a man remains in me and I in him, he will bear much fruit; apart from me you can do nothing."*

14.   James 1:22. *"Do not merely listen to the word, and so deceive yourselves. Do what is says."*

15.   Mark 10:45. *"For even the Son of man did not come to be*

served, but to serve, and to give his life as a ransom for many."

16. Colossians 3:23, NIV 1984. "Whatever you do, work at it with all your heart, as working for the Lord, not for men."

17. Luke 16:11. "So if you have not been trustworthy in handling worldly wealth, who will trust you with true riches?"

18. John 15:11. "I have told you this so that my joy may be in you and that your joy may be complete."

19. Matthew 22:37-39. "'Love the Lord your God with all your heart and with all your soul and with all your mind.' This is the first and greatest commandment. And the second is like it: 'Love your neighbor as yourself.'"

20. Romans 12:1, NASB. "Therefore I urge you, brethren, by the mercies of God, to present your bodies a living and holy sacrifice, acceptable to God, which is your spiritual service of worship."

21. Romans 12:2. "Do not conform to the pattern of this world, but be transformed by the renewing of your mind. Then you will be able to test and approve what God's will is – his good, pleasing and perfect will."

TRUTH

22. John 17:17. "Sanctify them by the truth; your word is truth."

23. John 14:6. "Jesus answered, 'I am the way and the truth and the life. No one comes to the Father except through me.'"

24. John 8:32. "Then you will know the truth, and the truth will set you free."

25. 2 Timothy 2:15. "Do your best to present yourself to God as one approved, a worker who does not need to be ashamed and who

correctly handles the word of truth."

26.   Psalm 40:11, NASB. "You, O Lord, will not withhold Your compassion from me; Your lovingkindness and Your truth will continually preserve me."

27.   Psalm 43:3, NLT. "Send out your light and your truth; let them guide me. Let them lead me to your holy mountain, to the place where you live."

28.   Psalm 119:43, ESV. "And take not the word of truth utterly out of my mouth, for my hope is in your rules."

29.   Ephesians 1:13. "And you also were included in Christ when you heard the message of truth, the gospel of your salvation. When you believed, you were marked in him with a seal, the promised Holy Spirit." 30.   Exodus 18:21, NASB. "Furthermore, you shall select out of all the people able men who fear God, men of truth, those who hate dishonest gain; and you shall place these over them as leaders of thousands, of hundreds, of fifties and of tens."

31.   Psalm 85:10, TLB. "Mercy and truth have met together. Grim justice and peace have kissed!"

32.   Luke 21:33. "Heaven and earth will pass away, but my words will never pass away."

33.   Hebrews 4:12. "For the word of God is alive and active. Sharper than any double-edged sword, it penetrates even to dividing soul and spirit, joints and marrow; it judges the thoughts and attitudes of the heart."

34.   2 Peter 1:21. "For prophecy never had its origin in the human will, but prophets, though human, spoke from God as they were carried along by the Holy Spirit."

35.   John 1:1-3. "In the beginning was the Word, and the Word

was with God, and the Word was God. He was with God in the beginning. Through him all things were made; without him nothing was made that has been made."

36. 2 Timothy 3:16-17. "All Scripture is God-breathed and is useful for teaching, rebuking, correcting and training in righteousness, so that the servant of God may be thoroughly equipped for every good work."

37. Joshua 1:8. "Do not let this Book of the Law depart from your mouth; meditate on it day and night, so that you may be careful to do everything written in it. Then you will be prosperous and successful."

38. 1 Timothy 2:15. "Do your best to present yourself to God as one approved, a worker who does not need to be ashamed and who correctly handles the word of truth."

39. Psalm 119:97. "Oh how I love your law! I meditate on it all day long."

40. Psalm 119:11. "I have hidden your word in my heart that I might not sin against you."

41. 1 Timothy 4:13. "Until I come, devote yourself to the public reading of Scripture, to preaching, and to teaching."

42. John 14:6. "I am the way and the truth and the life. No one comes to the Father except through me."

43. Philippians 2:5-11. "In your relationships with one another, have the same mindset as Christ Jesus: Who, being in very nature God, did not consider equality with God something to be used to his own advantage; rather, he made himself nothing by taking the very nature of a servant, being made in human likeness. And being found in appearance as a man, he humbled himself by becoming obe-

dient to death — even death on a cross! Therefore God exalted him to the highest place and gave him the name that is above every name, that at the name of Jesus every knee should bow, in heaven and on earth and under the earth, and every tongue acknowledge that Jesus Christ is Lord, to the glory of God the Father."

44.   Colossians 1:26-27. "the mystery that has been kept hidden for ages and generations, but is now disclosed to the Lord's people. To them God has chosen to make known among the Gentiles the glorious riches of this mystery, which is Christ in you, the hope of glory."

45.   Hebrews 1:1-4. "In the past God spoke to our ancestors through the prophets at many times and in various ways, but in these last days he has spoken to us by his Son, whom he appointed heir of all things, and through whom also he made the universe. The Son is the radiance of God's glory and the exact representation of his being, sustaining all things by his powerful word. After he had provided purification for sins, he sat down at the right hand of the Majesty in heaven. So he became as much superior to the angels as the name he has inherited is superior to theirs."

46.   John 16:13. "But when he, the Spirit of truth, comes, he will guide you into all the truth. He will not speak on his own; he will speak only what he hears, and he will tell you what is yet to come."

47.   Proverbs 15:22. "Plans fail for lack of counsel, but with many advisers they succeed."

48.   Romans 1:20. "For since the creation of the world God's invisible qualities — his eternal power and divine nature — have been clearly seen, being understood from what has been made, so that people are without excuse."

49.   Hebrews 11:1, NIV 1984: "Now faith is being sure of what we hope for and certain of what we do not see."

Faith

50.   Ephesians 2:8-9. "For it is by grace you have been saved, through faith – and this is not from yourselves, it is the gift of God – not by works, so that no one can boast."

51.   Mark 5:34. "He said to her, 'Daughter, your faith has healed you. Go in peace and be freed from your suffering.'"

52.   Hebrews 11:6. "And without faith it is impossible to please God, because anyone who comes to him must believe that he exists and that he rewards those who earnestly seek him."

53.   Matthew 13:58. "And he did not do many miracles there because of their lack of faith."

54.   Mark 9:23. "'If you can?' said Jesus. 'Everything is possible for one who believes.'"

55.   John 14:12. "Very truly I tell you, whoever believes in me will do the works I have been doing, and they will do even greater things than these, because I am going to the Father."

56.   Mark 11:24. "Therefore I tell you, whatever you ask for in prayer, believe that you have received it, and it will be yours."

57.   Luke 8:50. "Hearing this, Jesus said to Jairus, 'Don't be afraid; just believe, and she will be healed.'"

58.   Romans 3:22. "This righteousness is given through faith in Jesus Christ to all who believe. There is no difference between Jew and Gentile,"

59.   Romans 4:20-21. "Yet he did not waver through unbelief regarding the promise of God, but was strengthened in his faith and gave glory to God, being fully persuaded that God had power to do what he had promised."

60.   1 Corinthians 16:13. "Be on your guard; stand firm in the faith; be courageous; be strong."

61.   Galatians 3:9. "So those who rely on faith are blessed along with Abraham, the man of faith."

62.   2 Thessalonians 1:11. "With this in mind, we constantly pray for you, that our God may make you worthy of his calling, and that by his power he may bring to fruition your every desire for goodness and your every deed prompted by faith."

63.   2 Timothy 1:12. "That is why I am suffering as I am. Yet this is no cause for shame, because I know whom I have believed, and am convinced that he is able to guard what I have entrusted to him until that day."

64.   James 1:6. "But when you ask, you must believe and not doubt, because the one who doubts is like a wave of the sea, blown and tossed by the wind."

65.   James 2:26. "As the body without the spirit is dead, so faith without deeds is dead."

66.   James 5:15-16. "And the prayer offered in faith will make the sick person well; the Lord will raise them up. If they have sinned, they will be forgiven. Therefore confess your sins to each other and pray for each other so that you may be healed. The prayer of a righteous person is powerful and effective."

67.   Galatians 2:20. "I have been crucified with Christ and I no longer live, but Christ lives in me. The life I now live in the body, I live by faith in the Son of God, who loved me and gave himself for me."

68.   2 Corinthians 12:9-10. "But he said to me, 'My grace is sufficient for you, for my power is made perfect in weakness.' Therefore

I will boast all the more gladly about my weaknesses, so that Christ's power may rest on me. That is why, for Christ's sake, I delight in weaknesses, in insults, in hardships, in persecutions, in difficulties. For when I am weak, then I am strong."

69.   *1 Kings 18:39. "When all the people saw this, they fell prostrate and cried, "The Lord – he is God! The Lord – he is God!"*

70.   *Matthew 7:7-11. "Ask and it will be given to you; seek and you will find; knock and the door will be opened to you. For everyone who asks receives; the one who seeks finds; and to the one who knocks, the door will be opened. Which of you, if your son asks for bread, will give him a stone? Or if he asks for a fish, will give him a snake? If you, then, though you are evil, know how to give good gifts to your children, how much more will your Father in heaven give good gifts to those who ask him!"*

71.   *James 5:16-17, NKJV. "Therefore confess your sins to each other and pray for each other so that you may be healed. The prayer of a righteous person is powerful and effective. Elijah was a human being, even as we are. He prayed earnestly that it would not rain, and it did not rain on the land for three and a half years."*

72.   *Colossians 1:9-10. "For this reason, since the day we heard about you, we have not stopped praying for you. We continually ask God to fill you with the knowledge of his will through all the wisdom and understanding that the Spirit gives, so that you may live a life worthy of the Lord and please him in every way: bearing fruit in every good work, growing in the knowledge of God,"*

73.   *Psalm 109. From praise to petitions to praise.*

74.   *James 1:5-7. "If any of you lacks wisdom, you should ask God, who gives generously to all without finding fault, and it will be given to you. But when you ask, you must believe and not doubt,*

because the one who doubts is like a wave of the sea, blown and tossed by the wind. That person should not expect to receive anything from the Lord."

75.   Colossians 4:12-13. "Epaphras, who is one of you and a servant of Christ Jesus, sends greetings. He is always wrestling in prayer for you, that you may stand firm in all the will of God, mature and fully assured. I vouch for him that he is working hard for you and for those at Laodicea and Hierapolis."

Character

76.   Exodus 20:9-10. "Six days you shall labor and do all your work, but the seventh day is a sabbath to the Lord your God. On it you shall not do any work, neither you, nor your son or daughter, nor your male or female servant, nor your animals, nor any foreigner residing in your towns."

77.   1 Corinthians 6:19. "Do you not know that your bodies are temples of the Holy Spirit, who is in you, whom you have received from God? You are not your own;"

78.   1 Corinthians 12:3. "Therefore I want you to know that no one who is speaking by the Spirit of God says, 'Jesus be cursed,' and no one can say, 'Jesus is Lord,' except by the Holy Spirit."

79.   John 16:8-11. "When he comes, he will prove the world to be in the wrong about sin and righteousness and judgment: about sin, because people do not believe in me; about righteousness, because I am going to the Father, where you can see me no longer; and about judgment, because the prince of this world now stands condemned."

80.   Acts 8:29. "The Spirit told Philip, 'Go to that chariot and stay near it.'"

81.   Acts 13:2. "While they were worshiping the Lord and fast-

ing, *the Holy Spirit said, 'Set apart for me Barnabas and Saul for the work to which I have called them.'*"

82.   Galatians 5:25. *"Since we live by the Spirit, let us keep in step with the Spirit."*

83.   Ephesians 5:18-19. *"Do not get drunk on wine, which leads to debauchery. Instead, be filled with the Spirit, speaking to one another with psalms, hymns, and songs from the Spirit. Sing and make music from your heart to the Lord,"*

84.   1 Thessalonians 1:5. *"because our gospel came to you not simply with words but also with power, with the Holy Spirit and deep conviction. You know how we lived among you for your sake."*

85.   2 Timothy 3:16. *"All Scripture is God-breathed and is useful for teaching, rebuking, correcting and training in righteousness,"*

86.   John 14:26. *"But the Advocate, the Holy Spirit, whom the Father will send in my name, will teach you all things and will remind you of everything I have said to you."*

87.   Matthew 10:20. *"for it will not be you speaking, but the Spirit of your Father speaking through you."*

88.   Galatians 5:22-23. *"But the fruit of the Spirit is love, joy, peace, forbearance, kindness, goodness, faithfulness, gentleness and self-control. Against such things there is no law."*

CHAPTER 4. THE GREATEST CALLING – SERVING PEOPLE

89.   Mark 10:45. *"For even Jesus did not come to be served, but to serve, and to give his life as a ransom for many."*

90.   1 Peter 4:11. *"... if anyone serves, they should do so with*

the strength God provides."

91.   Isaiah 50:4, NASB. "*The Lord God has given Me the tongue of disciples, that I may know how to sustain the weary one with a word.*"

92.   Matthew 28:19. "*Therefore go and make disciples of all nations, baptizing them in the name of the Father and of the Son and of the Holy Spirit,*"

93.   Psalm 78:72, NASB. "*So he shepherded them according to the integrity of his heart, and guided them with his skillful hands.*"

94.   Proverbs 29:18, KJV. "*Where there is no vision, the people perish.*"

95.   Habakkuk 2:2, AMP. "*Write the vision and engrave it plainly on tablets so that the one who reads it may run.*"

96.   Hebrews 11:1, NIV 1984. "*Now faith is being sure of what we hope for and certain of what we do not see.*"

97.   Romans 15:13, NIV 1984. "*May the God of hope fill you with all joy and peace as you trust in him, so that you may overflow with hope by the power of the Holy Spirit.*"

98.   Luke 14:11. "*For everyone who exalts himself will be humbled, and he who humbles himself will be exalted.*"

99.   Ephesians 4:2. "*Be completely humble and gentle; be patient, bearing with one another in love.*"

100. James 4:10. "*Humble yourselves before the Lord, and he will lift you up.*"

101. Deuteronomy 8:2. "*Remember how the Lord your God led you all the way in the desert these forty years, to humble you and to test you in order to know what was in your heart, whether or not you*

would keep his commands."

102. Psalms 25:9. "He guides the humble in what is right and teaches them his way."

103. Matthew 22:37-39. "Love the Lord your God with all your heart and with all your soul and with all your mind . . . Love your neighbor as yourself."

104. Joshua 1:9. "Have I not commanded you? Be strong and courageous."

105. 1 Corinthians 16:13. "Be on your guard; stand firm in the faith; be courageous; be strong."

106. Ecclesiastes 4:12. "Though one may be overpowered, two can defend themselves. A cord of three strands is not quickly broken."

CHAPTER 5. THE HIGHEST STANDARD - PURSUING EXCELLENCE

107. 2 Corinthians 8:7. "But just as you excel in everything – in faith, in speech, in knowledge, in complete earnestness and in the love we have kindled in you – see that you also excel in this grace of giving."

108. Exodus 31:3. "I have filled him with the Spirit of God, with skill, ability and knowledge in all kinds of crafts."

109. Psalm 78:72, NASB. "So he shepherded them according to the integrity of his heart, and guided them with his skillful hands."

110. Proverbs 22:29, NIV 1996. "Do you see a man skilled in his work? He will serve before kings."

111. Ezekiel 28:5. "By your great skill in trading you have increased your wealth, and because of your wealth your heart has grown proud."

112. *Colossians 3:23.* *"Whatever you do, work at it with all your heart, as working for the Lord, not for human masters."*

113. *Mark 2 – Healing of the Paralytic Man*

114. *Matthew 7:7-8.* *"Ask and it will be given to you; seek and you will find; knock and the door will be opened to you. For everyone who asks receives; the one who seeks finds; and to the one who knocks, the door will be opened."*

115. *Proverbs 3:11-12.* *"My son, do not despise the Lord's discipline . . . because the Lord disciplines those he loves."*

116. *Proverbs 12:1.* *"Whoever loves discipline loves knowledge, but whoever hates correction is stupid."*

117. *Proverbs 14:23.* *"All hard work brings a profit, but mere talk leads only to poverty."*

118. *Proverbs 5:23.* *"For lack of discipline they will die, led astray by their own great folly."*

119. *Proverbs 10:17.* *"Whoever heeds discipline shows the way to life, but whoever ignores correction leads others astray."*

120. *Psalm 94:12.* *"Blessed is the one you discipline, Lord, the one you teach from your law."*

121. *Proverbs 23:13.* *"Do not withhold discipline from a child."*

122. *Proverbs 23:23, NIV 1996.* *"Buy the truth and do not sell it; get wisdom, discipline and understanding."*

123. *2 Tim 1:7, NIV 1996.* *"For God did not give us a spirit of timidity, but a spirit of power, of love and of self-discipline."*

124. *Proverbs 27:17.* *"As iron sharpens iron, so one person sharpens another."*

CHAPTER 6. THE ULTIMATE CAREER - STEWARDING RESOURCES

125. 1 Chronicles 29:11. "Yours, Lord, is the greatness and the power and the glory and the majesty and the splendor, for everything in heaven and earth is yours. Yours, Lord, is the kingdom; you are exalted as head over all."

126. Psalms 8:6. "You made them [man] rulers over the works of your hands; you put everything under their feet."

127. 1 Corinthians 4:2. "Now it is required that those who have been given a trust must prove faithful."

128. Philippians 4:12. "I know what it is to be in need, and I know what it is to have plenty. I have learned the secret of being content in any and every situation."

129. 2 Corinthians 9:6. "Whoever sows sparingly will also reap sparingly, and whoever sows generously will also reap generously."

130. Proverbs 22:7, NLT. "Just as the rich rule the poor, so the borrower is servant to the lender."

131. 1 Timothy 6:8. "But if we have food and clothing, we will be content with that."

132. Luke 18:18-23. "A certain ruler asked him, 'Good teacher, what must I do to inherit eternal life?' 'Why do you call me good?' Jesus answered. 'No one is good – except God alone. You know the commandments: "You shall not commit adultery, you shall not murder, you shall not steal, you shall not give false testimony, honor your father and mother."' 'All these I have kept since I was a boy,' he said. When Jesus heard this, he said to him, 'You still lack one thing. Sell everything you have and give to the poor, and you will have treasure in heaven. Then come, follow me.' When he heard this, he became *very sad, because he was very wealthy."*

133. 2 Corinthians 9:7. "You should give what you have decided in your heart to give."

134. Matthew 6:21. "For where your treasure is, there your heart will be also."

135. Philippians 2:3, NASB. " . . . but with humility of mind regard one another as more important than yourselves."

CHAPTER 7. THE NEW TRIPLE BOTTOM LINE – CREATING ECONOMIC, SOCIAL, AND SPIRITUAL CAPITAL

136. Genesis 2:15-18. "The Lord God took the man and put him in the Garden of Eden to work it and take care of it. And the Lord God commanded the man, 'You are free to eat from any tree in the garden; but you must not eat from the tree of the knowledge of good and evil, for when you eat of it you will surely die.' The Lord God said 'It is not good for the man to be alone. I will make a helper suitable for him.'"

137. Matthew 25:14-30 – The parable of the talents.

138. Proverbs 20:21, TLB. "Quick wealth is not a blessing in the end."

139. Proverbs 21:5, TLB. "Steady plodding brings prosperity; hasty speculation brings poverty."

140. Ecclesiastes 3:22. "So I saw that there is nothing better for a person than to enjoy their work, because that is their lot. For who can bring them to see what will happen after them?"

141. Matthew 22:36-39. "'Teacher, which is the greatest commandment in the Law?' Jesus replied: "Love the Lord your God with all your heart and with all your soul and with all your mind." This is the first and greatest commandment. And the second is like it: "Love your neighbor as yourself.""

142. Romans 13:8, NKJV. "Owe no one anything except to love one another, for he who loves another has fulfilled the law."

143. Judges 21:25, NASB. "In those days there was no king in Israel; everyone did what was right in his own eyes."

144. Philippians 4:8-9. "Finally, brothers and sisters, whatever is true, whatever is noble, whatever is right, whatever is pure, whatever is lovely, whatever is admirable – if anything is excellent or praiseworthy – think about such things. Whatever you have learned or received or heard from me, or seen in me – put it into practice. And the God of peace will be with you."

145. James 1:22, ESV. "But be doers of the word, and not hearers only, deceiving yourselves."

146. John 14:21, NIV 1984. "Whoever has my commands and obeys them, he is the one who loves me. He who loves me will be loved by my Father, and I too will love him and show myself to him."

CHAPTER 8. CALLED TO FLOURISH – LIVING THE ABUNDANT LIFE

147. Psalm 92:12, ESV. "The righteous flourish like the palm tree, and grow like a cedar in Lebanon. They are planted in the house of the Lord; they flourish in the courts of our God. They still bear fruit in old age."

148. Joshua 24:15, ESV. "And if it is evil in your eyes to serve the Lord, choose this day whom you will serve, whether the gods your fathers served in the region beyond the River, or the gods of the Amorites in whose land you dwell. But as for me and my house, we will serve the Lord."

149. Jeremiah 17:5–8. "This is what the Lord says: Cursed is the one who trusts in man, who draws strength from mere flesh and whose heart turns away from the Lord. That person will be like a bush in the wastelands; they will not see prosperity when it comes …. But blessed is the one who trusts in the Lord, whose confidence is in him. They will be like a tree planted by the water that sends out its roots by the stream. It does not fear when heat comes; its leaves are always green. It has no worries in a year of drought and never fails to bear fruit."

Dear Reader-

Thank you for being willing to persevere through this book. I hope that you are thinking differently about your purpose, passion and platform. Your journey to life-changing satisfaction is just beginning and I want you to know that www.HighImpactLIFE. com has amazing content to help you continue this journey.

Many readers have asked how they can contact me for an event or to share their thoughts.

☞ For speaking invitations, fill out the form at go.enterprisestewardship.com/let-us-help or email my team at connect@capitaliii.com.

☞ There are opportunities for new written and curated content at EnterpriseStewardship.com and on our social media sites.

☞ If you want more information about me, my businesses, other writing, or to see where I will be speaking, check www.PeteOchs.com.

☞ Finally, you can reach me at peteochs@capitaliii.com.

Have a blessed life!

Pete Ochs

www.EnterpriseStewardship.com
www.HighImpactLIFE.com
www.PeteOchs.com

About the Author

Pete Ochs is founder and chairman of Capital III, an impact investment company with investments in the US and Central America. Enterprise Stewardship is an initiative of Capital III that equips marketplace leaders with resources to transform their personal LIFE and business enterprises. During his four decades in business he has invested and operated companies in the energy, manufacturing, banking, and education sectors, oftentimes focusing on places devoid of human flourishing such as prisons and poverty-stricken countries. Pete's passion in life is to educate, equip, and empower business leaders around the world to live for something greater than themselves by using their business platform to impact the world for Christ.

Pete lives by four simple principles: Honor God; Serve People; Pursue Excellence; and Steward Capital. These four simple but powerful principles when brought to bear on creating Economic, Social and Spiritual Capital result in a High Impact LIFE.

Before launching his impact investment company Capital III, Pete spent 8 years in the commercial banking industry. Pete and his wife Debbie have been instrumental in founding and growing several nonprofit enterprises. They have two children and nine grandchildren.

Books presented by Enterprise Stewardship

A High Impact LIFE

Pete Ochs defines what it means to live a high impact life and provides today's leaders with the resources they need to define their purpose, embrace their passion, and maximize their platform for success in business and beyond.

978-1-64370-291-9

High Impact Habits

In this companion guide, Pete Ochs will guide you through your own transformation. This curriculum works you through eight life-changing lessons challenging you to know, believe, and do life differently.

978-1-64606-241-6

High Impact Wisdom

High Impact Wisdom is a daily devotional to help you recognize God's inspiration for a High Impact LIFE. Impactfully written by Boyd Bailey and Pete Ochs, this book is anchored with encouraging Scripture to help you gain a deeper appreciation for how to Love your Purpose, Live with Passion, and Leverage your Platform.

978-1-64786-080-6

High Impact Business

How do you become the steward God has entrusted you to be? *High Impact Business* will help you transform your business. It will make your STRATEGY visionary. It will make your OPERATIONS excellent. It will make your EXECUTION disciplined. But it will do much more than that. It will make your PURPOSE impactful.

978-1-63877-571-3

THE GOOD NEWS OF JESUS CHRIST

God Is Perfect – in Every Way!

The Rock! His work is *perfect*, for all His ways are justice. A God of *faithfulness* and *without iniquity, just* and *upright* is He.

Deuteronomy 32:4

Men & Women Are NOT Perfect

There is *none* righteous, no, *not one*; there is *none* who understands; there is *none* who seeks after God...for *all* have sinned and fallen short of the glory of God.

Romans 3:11, 23

God Requires Perfection

But as he who called you is holy, you also be holy *in all your conduct,* since it is written, "You shall be holy for I am holy."

1 Peter 1:15-16

Is There Any Hope? Yes! God Loves You Perfectly!

But God, being *rich in mercy*, because of *His great love* with which He loved us, even when we were *dead in our transgressions*, made us *alive together with Christ,* by grace you have been saved.

Ephesians 2:4-5

God's Action – HE Provided the Perfect Sacrifice!

He (Jesus) committed *no sin*, neither was deceit found in His mouth...He Himself *bore our sins* in His body on the tree, that we might die to sin and live to righteousness. By His wounds you have been healed.

> Peter 2:22, 24

Our Response – Repent and Believe

Have mercy on me, O God, according to your steadfast love; according to your abundant mercy blot out my transgressions. *Wash me thoroughly* from my iniquity and *cleanse me from my sin*! For I know my transgressions, and my sin is ever before me. Against you, you only, have I sinned and done what is evil in your sight.

> Psalm 51:1-4

New Life – Relationship with God

But to *all who did receive Him*, who *believed in His name*, He gave the right to become *children of God*. John 1:12

And he (Jesus) died for all, that those who live might no longer live for themselves but *for him* who for their sake *died* and was *raised*. Therefore, if anyone is *in Christ*, he is a *new creation*. The old has passed away; behold, the new has come. All this is from God, who through Christ *reconciled* us to Himself.

> 2 Corinthians 5:17-18

Notes

Notes

Notes

Notes

Notes

Notes